GOOD
FOOD
for BAD
DAYS

JACK MONROE

GOOD FOOD for BAD DAYS

bluebird
books for life

First published 2020 by Bluebird
an imprint of Pan Macmillan
The Smithson, 6 Briset Street, London EC1M 5NR

Associated companies throughout the world
www.panmacmillan.com

ISBN 978-1-5290-2818-8

9 8 7 6 5 4 3 2 1

A CIP catalogue record for this book is available from the British Library.
Typeset by Irissa Book Design
Printed and bound in Great Britain by CPI Books.

Visit www.panmacmillan.com to read more about all our books
and to buy them. You will also fin features, author interviews and
news of any author events, and you can sign up for e-newsletters
so that you're always firs to hear about our new releases.

Contents

Foreword

Food is emotional.

What we eat can impact our state of mind in all kinds of ways, and can conjure up pretty much every feeling known to human beings. We talk of food in emotional terms – 'comfort food' being the most obvious. Food doesn't just sustain our bodies, it is essential for our minds too. It can influence our health. When I had a full-blown breakdown, food became massively important, but also a massive challenge. I was well aware that if I wasn't eating properly, or enough, then I would feel even more rubbish, and yet cooking itself often seemed like a mountain to climb. When you are in a bad mental state, almost *anything* can seem a challenge. I can remember sitting on the end of my bed and taking about half an hour trying to decide which pair of socks to put on that day. Even when ninety per cent of the socks in the sock drawer were the same colour, it still seemed to take a Herculean effort.

The trouble is that when we most need to be eating well, we are often the least motivated to do so. When you are depressed you often have no energy and motivation. You even can feel you don't deserve to be looked after, even by yourself. When you are anxious you might have energy but it is not necessarily the energy that you need in the kitchen. It can often be the kind of energy that makes you pace around in circles and forget that you put the kettle on over an hour ago.

The thing is, good food doesn't have to be complicated food. Or inaccessible food. Good food is often the simplest food. When I was ill there was no simpler comfort than some toast with a thin spread of Marmite, followed by a more generous spread of peanut butter.

But the idea of cooking actual meals can seem like running a marathon. Anything that demands more than a toaster or a peel-off lid can seem like it is made for *other people*. And so, inadvertently, even the concept of fancy-pants recipes full of fancy-pants food can be another thing in the long list of Things That Make Us Feel Even More Useless.

Which is why having something like this book right here is such a blessing. No-nonsense, affordable, healthy and do-able recipes are precisely what you need when you are at your lowest. To stare at a long, overly fussy recipe can feel like trying to read a Russian novel at the best of times, so having a ready supply of simple, satisfying meals that are nourishing for the mind as well as the body – with easy-to-access foods – can be a real life raft through the choppier waters of life we sometimes find ourselves in.

This book will be a friend to you when life is hard. It offers no magic wand, but it will take some of the pain and stress out of feeding yourself. This book is a way to be kind to yourself, when it is not always easy to be kind to yourself. It is, in short, a blessing.

Thank goodness for Jack Monroe!

Matt Haig

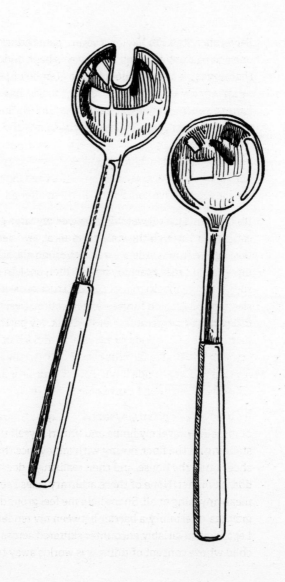

Introduction

September, 2019. I'm having a severe panic attack. Yes, another one. I'm partway through writing this book and suddenly I fear that none of it is good enough. The gremlin of perpetual negativity hisses that in fact none of it ever has been. *You're an imposssssssster*, it snarls, sounding not unlike Gollum from *Lord of the Rings*. I'm curled up on my enormous and seductively comfortable, if impractically pale blue, sofa, knees hunched into my chest, arms clenched around them, rocking gently, realizing with a soft bitterness that some of the tired old tropes about madness may have some truth in them after all.

It's 9.42 a.m. I'm still watching Cooper, my large ginger and white cat, glower through the voile curtains at my friend Ross who is tidying the front garden. I watch through glazed eyes, I despise myself, and I tear apart my half-written book in my head as I succumb to a maelstrom of self-destruction, self-loathing, sleepless nights and forgotten medication. Despite being sober for months, I desperately want a drink. My partner is at the hairdressers. It's a Friday. I'd have five and a half hours to sober up before having to face the school gates in the afternoon. I close my eyes and try to ride it out, rocking, rocking, as long as I don't move from this spot, I can't come to any harm.

It's 10:49 a.m. I open my eyes and gently, as though from outside of myself, unravel my limbs and unfurl myself until my feet are standing on the floor, noting with annoyance that I still have my shoes on in the house, and then realizing it doesn't matter. It doesn't matter. None of these arbitrary rules I set myself really mean anything at all. Shoes help me feel grounded. They add a gravitas, a certainty, a barrier between my tender soles and the Lego I will invariably encounter skittered across the floor by a child whose concept of tidiness is worlds away from my own.

I realize that doesn't matter either. 'Sorry about the mess, we were making memories instead' flits behind my eyes. A picture on someone else's wall. I note that I am sober and that I am calm. I don't know where I went for that hour; somewhere inside of myself, not awake and not asleep, not in chaos nor in peace, but elsewhere. And I am ready, I think to myself.

I pull my computer from my work bag and set it on my desk. I open it, take a deep breath, and know that it is time. I am four weeks and two days from the delivery of my first draft of this book. I make myself two double espressos from the fancy coffee machine I bought with the advance and set them beside my laptop. I line up my notebooks, three very specific pens and a bowl of boiled sweets beside me, and I breathe deeply, listening to the clock ticking in the silence until I can bear the suspense no longer. I have to do what I have to do, now, before I lose my nerve.

With just a moment's trepidation, I delete the entire manuscript and I start the whole damn thing again.

I'm Jack Monroe. You possibly know that, because my name is on the front of this book and if you're reading this, you probably clocked it. But I feel I should properly introduce myself, without all the fluff and PR that comes with a book cover of me smiling nicely in a clean shirt with my 'please buy me' eyes in.

I'm a cookbook author, writer, mother, inventor, creator, recovering alcoholic and I have chronic pain in my joints, especially in cold and damp weather. It's limiting, but it's also a fantastic excuse to carry an umbrella with a parrot's head for a handle and pretend to be Mary Poppins. Except my carpet bag is filled with three kinds of restricted drugs, as well as an EpiPen and a medical ID that instructs strangers on what to do and who to call if they find me. I also have depression, anxiety, severe adult ADHD, post-traumatic stress disorder and that old friend to women who achieve anything at all: imposter syndrome. I talk about some of this some of the time, but I've long learned that it's important to direct my own narrative and tell my own story, rather than have to worry about being 'outed' by the tabloid press. So here we are. I'm officially absolutely batshit bonkers, and what started off as a slight chemical imbalance in childhood was watered by the poisoned can of poverty and has since grown into quite the gnarly jungle.

I have survived violence, poverty, traumas I won't describe in great detail for fear of triggering anyone who has experienced similar. I have moved house twenty-four times, mostly in terrible circumstances but more recently in happier ones, and long may that be the case. I'm also a public speaker, giving talks on alleviating poverty and resolving individual difficulties with dignity, and the impact that one person can have on another person's life. I cook on television sometimes, have half a million followers across varying social media platforms, and have recently ventured into YouTube – mostly reading recipes aloud as bedtime stories, but occasionally daring myself to sing. I'm a loyal if disorganized friend, generous to the point of troublesome, and despite a decade of difficult experiences, I still gasp in wonder at the crash of a wave on a rock, an unexpected butterfly, or a supermarket markdown on the fancy cheeses.

The idea for this book came from a recipe I wrote on Instagram a few years ago, called Self Love Stew. Essentially just a pile of miscellany thrown into a pot on a bad day, I dispensed with my usual recipe-writing patter and tapped out a soliloquy of frustration, fury and distress, peppered with scant cooking instructions and finished with a shoulders-down sigh of relief and a whisper to myself that it might just be okay. That recipe was so popular, I put it in my book *Cooking on a Bootstrap*, and on my website, and it's still one of the ones that people send me photographs of the most on Instagram and Twitter. I wonder if I could do a whole book like this, I mused to myself, and pitched it to my publisher, Carole. Originally titled 'Depressipes' (yes, I am very pleased with that term, so much so I trademarked it in a fit of excitement), I wanted to write a manual for nourishing yourself when it's the last thing you feel like doing. We agreed that 'Depressipes', although a great word, didn't quite encompass or communicate the book as it was when finished, so we called it *Good Food For Bad Days* instead. It's the book I've been most nervous about, because in places it is raw, unapologetic, uncompromising and bleak, but also beautiful, encouraging and, hopefully, a reliable friend to keep in the kitchen to coax you to take care of yourself in simple ways.

I've not been shy about talking about my mental health in public; speaking openly and candidly about struggling with going from being a single mum on the dole to a very minor media personality, and the trolls and abuse that seem to come hand in hand with being a woman with an opinion. I've written about a childhood eating disorder that extended well into my late teens, about anxiety, post-traumatic stress, and more. I want this book to be a companion, rather than a misery memoir, a set footprint that you can step into, hopefully comforted with the knowledge that this is a path that has been trodden some way before. I don't have all the answers – I'm afraid I am just winging it, hour by hour, day by day – but I do have some cracking delicious and very simple dinners, and that's usually a pretty good place to start.

Fuelling Your Reserve Tank

I'm not here to make any wild claims about 'healing' or 'curing' yourself with various foods, because if it were that simple, someone would already have smashed all these so-called superfoods together into a handy tiny pill and – bam! – our brain chemicals would all be hunky-dory again. And the reason why that handy tiny pill doesn't exist is because there's no one miracle food out there that can singlehandedly realign the complex combination of chemistry, environment, make-up, experiences and all the other factors that can contribute to poor mental health.

That said, I have been in therapy over the last two years (and I can highly recommend it; having been initially sceptical to the point of churlish, I can only say I wish I had been less pig-headed and frightened about it and done it far sooner), and it's not a case of prostrating myself on a chaise longue and weeping about my childhood. It's about finding coping mechanisms and positive routines to underpin the hustle and horror of the everyday. I have both autism and ADHD, which, even without a litany of traumatic and difficult experiences peppered throughout my formative years, makes 'human-ing' quite tricky sometimes. Remembering to eat, to clean myself, to stick to appointments, can be a minefield. Time is elastic; I'm either wading through treacle or spinning wildly out of kilter. I frequently double-book events or forget where I'm meant to be, or dash off sweary apologetic emails as I'm running an hour late to a crucial work meeting. I burn up, flake out, cancel on friends frequently, can spend days on end not leaving the house.

I've started to get better over the last year, by putting some systems in place. Foundations. Literal checklists of things to do every single day that, as far as I can work out, most people just seem to intrinsically know how to do. I must have skipped that bit in the programming queue, because I have to actively check these off on a list every day. Eat breakfast. Shower. Brush teeth. Put clean clothes on. Make bed. Check emails. Prioritize work tasks. Plan work day. Eat lunch. Et cetera, et cetera. I like order and structure. On the face of it, people see my alphabetized 100-strong spice rack, or the kitchen utensil rack organized by core function, or the colour-blocked wardrobe, labelled bookshelves, fanatically folded t-shirts and marvel at how organized I am. It's a thin veneer of respectability, a translucent film holding together the junk and chaos at my core.

I'm not remotely organized really. I'm an absolute ruin. I just know how to roll up towels nicely because I briefly worked on the towel aisle of a supermarket. Nicely rolled towels can deflect from a multitude of things, by the way. I recommend it. But my default setting is disruption, destruction and disarray. So I have systems in place, to keep some sort of structure in my world. Left to my own devices, I would be drunk to the point of comatose, sleeping on a pile of newspapers, surrounded by empty yoghurt pots and saved butter dishes 'just in case'. I have 183 clean, rinsed jars hoarded in a kitchen cupboard and under the stairs. This organization is born of a fear – in itself a knowledge of what happens when chaos is allowed to reign.

And so, when I started to attend therapy sessions, I realized I needed mental systems to keep my disordered mind in check, the same way as I had implemented physical systems to keep my disordered home tidy. Luckily for me, my therapist, Duncan, is familiar with autism and ADHD, and we started to work out ways of implementing some mental structure and support day to day. One of the most successful that I have found, I refer to as 'keeping the reserve tank full'. Bear with me, this is going somewhere. When I first walked through Duncan's door, I was an absolute shambles of a human being. Regularly drunk, stuttering, shrunken, gaze fixed on some imaginary stain on the carpet, sullen and deeply sad for reasons I couldn't begin to describe. I was convinced that I, as a human being, was a lost cause. And we had to start from the beginning. Making me into a functional human, most of the time, was all I wanted from this hourly arrangement. I quickly realized that that wasn't how it worked. Duncan didn't have a snappy solution, and this was going to be a process, rather than an instant exorcism. It was about finding a communal language and workable daily habits that we could incorporate into my chaotic and disordered life, in order to start to develop some structure and self-esteem. I tried a few different things – and the Reserve Tank, as it is affectionately known, is the one that stuck.

All of our reserve tanks will look completely different. It's the baseline of daily things that keep our little worlds spinning madly on. Common denominators for having a mostly good day. A shopping list of the absolute fundamentals required in order for me, or you, to start to thrive. My list is achievably short, but I try to make sure I do it every single day. Have a wash. Make my bed. Remember to take my medication and vitamins. Eat at least two decent, healthy meals. Drink plenty of fluids. Wear clean clothes.

One of the other things on my Reserve Tank list is to eat at least three things off the following list every day. This I created with all the caveats that there is no one superfood that can 'cure' bad days, but there *is* some pretty solid scientific backing for including the following foods to support healthy brain function and boost your mood. It's not going to give you immunity to depression, self-loathing or miscellaneous terrible life events, but it might give you a slightly more solid foundation from which you can start to deal with them. Or it might not. But it's worth a go.

FOODS TO CONSIDER EATING REGULARLY, AND SOME REASONS WHY YOU SHOULD

BANANAS contain tryptophan, which is a kind of amino acid. Tryptophan is converted by vitamin B6 into serotonin, a naturally occurring hormone made in our body that plays a role in regulating mood and our sleep. Boosting serotonin may help keep 'the blues' at bay.

BEANS AND PULSES are a good source of amino acids, which are the building blocks of proteins. Your brain uses certain amino acids to help regulate moods and feelings. Beans are a source of protein and fibre and so may help you stay full, meaning you are less likely to want to crave quick-fix sugary snacks.

BREAKFAST CEREALS are often fortified with the mineral calcium and while we tend to associate calcium with strong bones and teeth, some research suggests that if you don't get enough calcium you may also be at risk for depression.[1]

CHEESE can help to increase tryptophan intake, which supports normal serotonin production. Tryptophan also helps us to make melatonin, which is a hormone released in response to light levels that helps us to start the process of falling asleep.

CHICKEN is a source of tryptophan as well as tyrosine, another amino acid that supports normal production of serotonin, a hormone made in our body that plays a role in regulating mood and our sleep.

CHOCOLATE is made with cocoa solids and these contain a natural derivative of caffeine called theobromine. This in combination with the fats and sugar used in chocolate is thought to give its mood-enhancing effects as shown in research.[2] Just one small square, especially dark chocolate, might be enough to give you a little 'lift' during the day.

LENTILS contain complex carbohydrates and these can help stabilize blood sugar levels, which may help to 'level out' our energy levels and have a knock-on effect to our moods. Lentils are also high in folate, which may help to prevent the incidence of depression, although the mechanism for this is not clear yet.[3] Finally, lentils are a source of iron, for normal energy release.

NUTS are rich in selenium – especially Brazil nuts, eat just three of them to help you meet your selenium needs for the day. It is thought by some researchers that not getting enough selenium might increase the rate of depression.[4]

OATS have a medium glycaemic index (GI) reading, meaning that they have a slower effect on our blood glucose (sugars) levels when we eat them. Eating more low and medium GI foods helps stabilize energy levels by keeping our blood sugars and, in turn, our mood stable. Oats also contain some selenium (see nuts entry above).

OILY FISH is a good source of omega 3 fatty acids. Growing research indicates that a deficiency in these essential fatty acids may increase susceptibility to depression and low mood, so it's well worth trying to eat a bit more 'fatty' fish.[5] These fatty acids form a large percentage of our brain tissue. Try to eat salmon, mackerel and sardines. Keep tinned varieties handy for speedy, low-effort snacks.

OYSTERS aren't on my list as I am violently allergic to them, but they are a good source of zinc, which is needed for normal brain function. Three oysters contain 100% of your recommended daily intake of zinc and the tinned variety you can get in the supermarket are just as good as fresh ones.

LEAFY GREEN VEG such as spinach, kale, swiss chard, collard greens and cruciferous vegetables such as broccoli and brussels sprouts have B vitamins in abundance. Sufficient levels of the B vitamins: thiamine (vitamin B1), niacin (vitamin B3), cobalamin (vitamin B12) and pyridoxine (vitamin B6) are needed for normal psychological function.

TOFU, made from fermented soy beans, is often known as a good source of calcium and protein but it also contains tryptophan, an amino acid needed in the production of serotonin.

WATER Staying hydrated is vital for our minds and bodies to function properly. Therefore, being dehydrated can have a huge impact on both our mental and physical health and our ability to concentrate. I fill up three 750ml drinking bottles every morning, one with juice, one with cold sweetened chamomile tea and one with water, making sure that I drink them by the end of the day. It's an easy way to make sure I get 2 litres a day and then a bit more for good measure.

WHOLE GRAINS are rich in tryptophan, which helps produce serotonin and melatonin. Serotonin helps regulate our moods and melatonin plays a role in initiating sleep. Whole grains are rich in fibre and complex carbohydrates which can help to maintain a steady blood sugar level and this in turn, can help stabilize our moods.

Your Food First Aid Kit

I deliberately try to keep these lists as short as possible because my cookery ethos is to teach the most people I can to feed themselves the best they can, with the least they have available, so honking great big lists of ingredients and gadgets don't belong here. That said, here are a few things that make throwing a meal together from scratch on a bad day almost bearable. They're by no means essential, but they could be useful ...

FAIRLY ESSENTIAL INGREDIENTS

A JAR OF ASSORTED STOCK CUBES. I can't emphasize enough how important stock cubes are to create base flavours; even the most basic ones from the supermarket impart a tiny powerhouse of flavour to underpin everything else. I use them in soups, curries, risottos, sometimes even in mac and cheese. There's nothing shameful about using a stock cube instead of fresh stock, despite the fashion for boiling up vats of bones. It's a pinch of culinary magic – saline, sweet and gorgeously golden – so use with abandon. Nobody's going to judge you here.

A BASIC DRESSING. Mix equal parts fat and acid – yes, even sunflower oil and white vinegar – and use this as a simple dressing to inject some life into a savoury dish that falls flat. This little trick enlivens even the blandest of casseroles or soups, so bung a dressing in a jar, shake it up and stick it in the fridge.

FROZEN FRUIT. Whizz it up with some milk and oats for a quick breakfast smoothie, or stir it into a yoghurt before you go to bed and surprise yourself with ready made breakfast in the morning. I sometimes microwave frozen fruit until it's a hot, sloppy compote and dump a tin of custard on the top. Either way, it's a swift injection of vitamins, suspended in ice to keep them peppy and good for you, and absolutely delicious.

SAUERKRAUT. Have it on crackers with a sloppy dip like hummus or cottage cheese, stir it through a soup to liven it up, or just eat it with your fingers. It's cheap, good for you, and a little goes a long way.

SAGE AND ONION STUFFING. Use it dry, straight from the packet, as a thickener for soups, a crunch on top of your lasagne or sprinkle it onto a cheesy pasta like fancy breadcrumbs, or make it up and roll it into dumplings. I keep a jar of several decanted packets next to my microwave and often surprise myself at where it ends up. Oh, it's great for binding slightly wet burgers, too.

A POT NOODLE. No, really. I keep a Bombay Bad Boy in the back of my cupboard for truly blue days, then just jazz it up with a tablespoon of peanut butter and a fistful of small diced frozen veg. It's filling, punchy, and if you pack it with veggies, it's almost good for you.

And on that note, you could do worse than keeping some instant soup sachets to hand to make quick pasta sauces with (I like the Ainsley Harriott Szechuan pepper one over noodles with frozen veg, personally), and a few varieties of microwavable rice. Because if you're bothering to cook yourself a main meal from scratch, you deserve to cheat on your rice. I almost always do, and I cook for a living, so you can too.

FAIRLY ESSENTIAL EQUIPMENT

I've deliberately tried to keep these recipes as simple as possible, so this equipment list is short but can be added to over time, if you like. These are things that I find help me on particularly low-energy days, and make cooking a lot quicker and simpler.

A SMALL BULLET BLENDER. I picked mine up from Wilko's, a large hardware and department store that has many branches throughout the UK, and also a wide delivery area online. Most supermarkets now have their own-brand versions of small bullet-style blenders too, so there's no need to splash out on the high-end versions. I vigorously road test mine at approximately ten times the usage of the average household kitchen, and they have lasted me around three years each – and I am haphazard, forgetful, clumsy and irreverent about it, so they should last you much longer! Brilliant for knocking up quick smoothies, soups from tatty old vegetables, dips, salsas, pâtés and more, I couldn't live without mine now.

A VEGETABLE DICER. I call this the VegHammer, because of its propensity for smashing even the gnarliest of swedes and celeriacs into neat little cubes. Just slice your veg around a centimetre thick – I use a bread knife for the tough stuff, and leave the skin on – then bang it through one of these. It's like having an apprentice chef beside you carefully chopping all your vegetables into neat little squares. I recommend the OXO Good Grips one, as it's designed specifically for arthritic or less-mobile joints.

A BREAD KNIFE. I have become evangelical in recent years about a bread knife being pretty much the only knife you need in the kitchen. Ideal for slicing through the toughest of squashes or swedes, jointing meat and slicing bread, there's not much it can't do. And because it's serrated, it never needs to be sharpened. I have a drawer of around sixty knives in my kitchen these days, and the bread knife is the only one that ever sees the light of day 90 per cent of the time.

SOME TUPPERWARE CONTAINERS, LABELS AND A PERMANENT MARKER. Ideal for storing leftovers or batch cooking and then labelling them so you know what they are! It sounds simple, and I guess it is, but having neat little labels on my homemade ready meals means I'm much more likely to actually eat them than play freezer roulette – and when the gremlins descend or when the freezer starts to get full, I write a list on the front of the fridge of what there is, and tell the family to help themselves and sort their own meals out for a few days while I retreat with my Pot Noodles into darkness somewhere.

As a teenager, I used to hang around in bookshops in my local high street, as a kind of refuge from a house full of fostered children – who I adored, but living in the epicentre of a revolving door of trauma did sometimes take its toll. I disappeared into books – fiction and non-fiction, classics, cookery, poetry, travel – anything I could get my hands on and bury my eyes in.

When I started to earn my own money, at the age of fifteen working in a fish and chip shop, I started to purchase my own books – most of which I no longer have, as poverty forced me to sell every single thing I owned in the summer of 2012, down to almost every book, every mug, every plate, every lampshade – but I have rebuilt my collection from scratch in the years that followed.

One book that didn't sell, because nobody wanted to buy it, was a dishevelled copy of *Notes From Underground* by Fyodor Dostoyevsky. Crinkly from being dropped in the bath and dried out on a radiator, I was secretly relieved, because although I had owned it for around five years by this point, I hadn't finished it. I still haven't, and it's getting on for thirteen years old now, which must be some kind of record. I read a few pages at a time and then had to stop, his depictions of darkness and mania and paranoia too close to my bones for me to allow myself to take in too much of it at any one time.

One line, however, has stuck with me – 'Let the world go to Hell, but I should always have my tea.'

This chapter embodies that sentiment, not just with tea, but with varying warm comforts in short receptacles, designed to be cupped in your hands, held with a casual abandon or curled up in a corner with. Sometimes all you need is a mug of soup or bashed-up boiled eggs with butter to ground yourself in the middle of your own cupped hands, with no formalities, just a moment's pause in the storm.

MUGS

Liquid Gold VE

MAKES 1 LITRE

50g fresh root ginger

a knob of fresh turmeric, or 1 tbsp of the ground stuff

60ml lemon juice, fresh or bottled

6 whole cloves

½ tsp black peppercorns, or mixed

¼ tsp cayenne pepper

1 tsp ground cinnamon

honey or other liquid sweetener of your choice, to taste

I make a large pot of this when I am feeling under the weather, or caring for someone else who is, and it truly feels like a magical potion. Much has been written about the anti-inflammatory properties of curcumin, the active ingredient in turmeric, and although it probably isn't quite the miracle cure for everything that certain corners of the internet would have you believe, it definitely does some good when my body is ailing, and that's good enough for me. The ginger here helps settle the stomach and ease digestion, and the peppers add a gentle pep of heat – how gentle depends on how heavy handed you are with the cayenne, so season accordingly!

First, peel and chop your ginger and turmeric as finely as you can, then toss it into a large heavy-bottomed saucepan. Add the lemon juice and cloves and measure in the peppercorns, cayenne pepper and cinnamon. Pour over a litre of water, then stir in the honey or other liquid sweetener of your choice. Bring to the boil, then reduce to a simmer on the smallest hob ring, for 20 minutes.

Remove from the heat and stand it to one side for an hour to continue to infuse, and to cool completely. I pour mine into an empty squash bottle once it has started to cool down, with the lid screwed on tightly.

Strain the gubbins out and set the strained liquid to one side – see opposite for a tip on how not to waste all the bits! Pour the liquid back into the cleaned bottle and drink throughout the day, warm or cold.

GOOD FOOD FOR BAD DAYS

TIPS

- *For a creamier drink, reduce the liquid by half with a vigorous boil, then warm it through with full-fat coconut milk or other heavy milk of your choice.*

- *When straining the liquid, I can't bring myself to throw away such a quantity of ginger, so I pick out the roots and the cloves and use them in daal, where the added spices bring a pleasant base note to the party.*

- *If you have a slow cooker, you could place all of the ingredients in it and set it to Low for 6 hours to properly infuse and steep.*

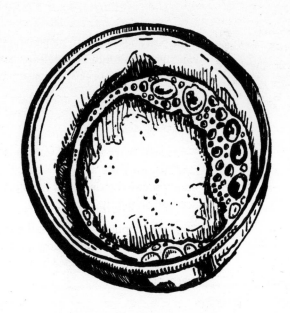

Honey Nut Milk v

MAKES AROUND 570ML

50g honey or other liquid sweetener of your choice

100g your favourite peanut butter

450ml whole or semi-skimmed milk

I first had peanut milk at a small cafe called BAO, on Lexington Street, Soho. Hot, sweet, sticky bao buns were served with tall glasses of ice-cold peanut milk – I slurped mine in seconds and ordered two more. Traditionally nut milks are made by soaking nuts overnight in cold water, then blending them and straining through a muslin cloth or nut milk bag. I can do that, and indeed I have done, but this method is much faster and thus, instantly gratifying. To make this vegan, use a creamy plant-based milk of your choice and replace the honey with maple, golden or agave syrup.

I'll warn you now, it's completely addictive, and that's fine because, despite its relatively high calorie content, it's a good source of protein and natural sugars. I can drink this by the pint, and I defy you not to, too.

Weigh your honey and peanut butter into the large cup of a bullet blender or the jug of a standard blender, and measure in the milk. Blend for 30 seconds, then pause briefly, before blending for 30 seconds more.

It should be a completely smooth liquid, but in case of stray pieces of peanut, place a fine-mesh sieve on top of a large bowl or pan and pour the milk through it to strain.

Carefully pour the milk into a jar, bottle or empty milk bottle, seal and store in the fridge for up to 4 days.

Tea Shandy VE

**MAKES 1 LITRE,
QUANTITIES EASILY
ADJUSTED**

2 herbal or
flavoured tea bags

500ml boiling water

500ml lemonade

I make this for myself very regularly as an alternative to alcoholic drinks when hosting friends for lunch or dinner, or just for something lightly sparkling and pleasantly grown-up to drink of an evening. It works with any kind of lemonade and any kind of tea, so the possibilities are endless. My favourite is a light floral tea, like rose or jasmine, steeped strong and served chilled, but all varieties seem to work beautifully.

Boil your kettle and pop the tea bags in a heatproof measuring jug. Cover with boiling water to make 500ml, stir vigorously, and leave to stand for 10–15 minutes to infuse. Remove the tea bags and allow the tea to cool – I speed up this process by adding ice cubes and stirring them in before popping the jug in the fridge.

When cool, pour into a 1 litre bottle or divide evenly between two 500ml bottles, and top up with lemonade. Return to the fridge to chill and drink within 3 days.

Sleepy Hot Chocolate v

MAKES 1 X 500G
JAR

1 tbsp dried rose
petals

1 tbsp dried lavender
flowers

1 tsp vanilla powder
(optional)

125g sugar of your
choice

125g dark cocoa
powder

250g coconut milk
powder or skimmed
milk powder

I make a mug of this subtly scented hot chocolate and take it to bed with me to drink myself to sleep with – a sentence I once would have used about a bottle of whisky, but I now satisfy myself with warm, floral hot chocolate instead. I first made it by steeping whole lavender and rose petals in warm milk and making it into hot chocolate, but I would get them stuck to my teeth if I didn't strain it properly, and sometimes only instant gratification will do.

Measure the rose petals and lavender flowers into the small cup of a bullet blender and add the vanilla, if using, and the sugar. Pulse to a very fine powder.

Pass the ground powder through a fine-mesh sieve to catch any large pieces of rose and lavender. You can re-blend it if there is a lot left, to get the best from it.

Transfer the scented sugar to a large airtight jar and measure in the cocoa powder and coconut milk powder or skimmed milk powder. Seal the lid and shake well to evenly distribute the ingredients.

To make it into a hot drink, boil the kettle and spoon 4 rounded tablespoons into your favourite mug. Add a splash of boiled water and stir well to make it a thick paste, then thin with a slow trickle of water, stirring continuously for best results. Top up with a dash of milk if you fancy an even creamier taste, or a smattering of marshmallows – or both!

Golden Milk V

400ml light
coconut milk

200ml any milk

2 tsp ground
turmeric

½ tsp ground ginger

½ tsp ground
cinnamon

a few pinches of
black pepper

2 tbsp honey or
other liquid
sweetener of your
choice, to taste

Golden milk is based on an old ayurvedic recipe called Haldi Doodh. In its simplest form, it is warm milk with turmeric. Combining turmeric with black pepper and a healthy fat like coconut oil increases its bioavailability, which is a scientific term for how quickly something is absorbed into the body's circulatory system. In layman terms, it means you get more bang for your curcumin buck by combining all three. On cold, damp days, when my joints start to ache, I make a vat of this in a 1 litre slow cooker that sits in the corner of my office and drink it throughout the day. The gently spiced, warming mug may be a placebo effect, but all the same, it certainly makes me feel a little better – and it tastes delicious, too. To make it vegan, use your favourite plant-based milk – cashew and almond both work beautifully here – and swap the honey for a liquid sweetener of your choice.

Warm the coconut milk and milk together in a medium saucepan, then add the spices and honey, or other sweetener of choice. Simmer for 10 minutes, stirring occasionally, until the milk is a deep golden colour.

Drink immediately, or it keeps for 2–3 days in the fridge. It can be enjoyed cold, but warm through to serve for best results.

Hot Nurse VE

SERVES 4, OR 1
POORLY PERSON
ALL THROUGH
THE DAY

6 fat cloves of garlic

a knob of fresh
ginger, peeled

2 x 400g tins of
chopped tomatoes

1 tbsp medium curry
powder

1 tsp ground
turmeric

salt and pepper, to
taste

This recipe is known as Hot Nurse in my household for its ability to flush out a blocked-up nose, soothe a sore throat, chase away a hangover and revitalize my tired head. It is a real kick in the cookies, as my mum used to say; so those of you who choose the mild curries in restaurants may want to halve the ginger and curry powder quantities. For the rest of you, ladle it into a mug and take your medicine! I keep a supply of it in the freezer in microwave-proof containers, for emergencies, and I sip it through the winter to keep snuffles and grumbles at bay.

The easiest way to make this soup is to pop the garlic, ginger and tomatoes into a blender – don't add the curry powder and turmeric, as they will stain – and blast to a pulp. Pour into a saucepan and add the curry powder, turmeric and salt and pepper. Bring to a gentle simmer. Fill one of the empty tomato tins with water and pour into the pan, then cook for 25 minutes, stirring so it doesn't stick and burn at the bottom.

If you are an 'early taster', like me, and can't resist dipping a spoon in every few minutes, the first few tastes will be shockingly tangy with garlic and ginger – this cooks out and mellows, so don't be alarmed!

I leave mine to cool for an hour after cooking to really temper the ginger–garlic heat, then warm it through to serve.

Will keep in the fridge for 3 days, or the freezer for 3 months.

Eggy Cup V

MAKES 1 CUP

3 large or
4 medium eggs

1 tbsp butter

a generous pinch
of salt

plenty of black
pepper

It's 1999, or thereabouts. I am lying on the sofa in my parents' family home, eleven or twelve years old and already beginning to feel exhausted by everyday life. I'm not like other girls; not in the manic, pixie-dream, girl trope of the selfish Hollywood protagonist, but acutely aware of my difference without being able to give it a name. I get distracted, I talk too loudly. I finish my work quickly and then become disruptive, eager to be liked, to be laughed with or at – any form of validation is fine. I complain of a headache, a stomach ache, unable to express that really, I just ache. My mum brings me a green mug and a sympathetic look, interrupting my pity party, and I pull myself up to a sitting position and gratefully accept it. It's our thing, a secret pick-me-up for days when we need a little comfort and care.

As an adult, I still make myself an eggy cup when I'm feeling blue. It requires very little effort to cobble together and stands up as a decent meal. You could jazz it up by adding sautéed vegetables, if you like, a fistful of finely sliced leafy greens or gently wilted spinach or kale, but I love it for its kindergarten simplicity, the comforting simultaneous richness and blandness of every spoonful and, most of all, the deeply held memory of the warmth of my mother's love, moment by moment, mug by mug.

RECIPE OVER THE PAGE →

Bring a medium pan of water to the boil and carefully place each egg into it, making sure that there is enough water in the pan to completely submerge them. Set a timer for 4 minutes exactly – I use the stopwatch on my phone – and reduce the heat to a simmer. If using medium eggs, set your timer for 3 minutes and 50 seconds. It may seem pernickety, but it works.

Fill a bowl, or separate pan, with water as cold as you can muster. You may add ice cubes if you have them, but they aren't strictly essential. When the eggs have boiled for the set amount of time, remove them swiftly from the pan with a spoon and carefully transfer them into the cold water. This both halts the cooking process and shocks the internal membrane into coming away from the eggshell, making them easier to peel. Stand the eggs in the cold water for half a minute, until easy to handle.

Peel the eggs one by one, discarding the shells, and drop them into a large mug. Add the butter, salt and pepper, and mash with a fork until it's a hot buttery mess. Eat immediately, preferably somewhere comfortable and soothing, or hand it to someone you care for as a silent 'I love you'. Leftovers will keep in the fridge for 24 hours, but do cover the mug with film or foil as it may stink out your fridge!

Addendum: I sent my mum this recipe for approval and she reminded me that she slices the tops off the boiled eggs and scoops the insides out, as it's easier than peeling them. So you could do that instead. Mum also reminds me that this, with a very finely chopped raw onion in, was a family favourite sandwich filling for beach days and picnics, so you could make an enormous batch of it and do that, too. The beach is optional but highly recommended.

My dad was a Paratrooper, before he was a firefighter and foster carer and first aid teacher, and those of you who have been similarly raised by an ex-military parent may identify with some aspects of my childhood. Specifically, the ability to be able to polish and bull a pair of shoes, make hospital corners with flat sheets, and you may be familiar with the phrase: 'proper preparation prevents piss-poor performance', which was barked at me and my siblings on a near-daily basis.

When I have worked in restaurant kitchens, a similar concept is known as *mise en place*, which is French for 'things in place', or, as a layperson may say: 'prep'. *Mise en place* usually refers to the setting up of ingredients and equipment to make the running of the kitchen smooth and efficient, and can range from chopping vegetables, to ensuring everything you need is to hand, and to making some of the component parts of a dish in advance so it is easier to pull together in a busy service shift.

I use the term *mise en place* at home (pretty much in the same way as my dad would machine-gun a patter of p-words at me) to refer to any handy pots I keep in the fridge. It's not done following it in its strictest term, but it's my home, so I'll do what I like. The recipes that follow are useful for keeping on standby, to be made in a lucid or organized moment, so that when I'm tired, or busy, or have just forgotten to feed myself, I can bang something together in under a minute with little to no effort at all.

HANDY POTS

Tuna and Chilli Rillette

MAKES 1 DECENT-SIZED JAR

2 spring onions

a little parsley (optional)

200g tinned tuna, in oil

100g soft cream cheese

½ tsp chilli flakes

2 tbsp bottled lemon or lime juice

salt and pepper, to taste

A rillette is a rough pâté, coarse and usually served at room temperature with bread and pickles. This tuna version is a way of ekeing out a small can of fish to serve a few, and making it a little more interesting in the process. Almost any canned fish works here, so feel free to use whatever you have to hand or according to personal preference.

First chop your spring onions and parsley, if using, very finely, into minuscule pieces, with a large heavy knife. Transfer to a large mixing bowl.

Drain most of the oil from the tuna, reserving it in a bowl, as you will add a little back in shortly. Tip the tuna into the mixing bowl. Spoon in the cream cheese, and measure in the chilli flakes. Add the lemon or lime juice, and mix well to combine.

Add a little of the reserved oil, and mix to combine. Continue until you achieve your desired consistency; I like mine butter-soft and slightly sloppy, but you may prefer it a little thicker.

Season to taste with salt and pepper, and store in a sealed clean jar or container in the fridge. It will keep for 3 days. Do not freeze.

GOOD FOOD FOR BAD DAYS

Peanut Butter Hummus V

MAKES 1 DECENT-SIZED TUB

400g tin of chickpeas

1 or 2 cloves of garlic, depending on tolerance

3 tbsp light cooking oil

1–2 tbsp peanut butter, to taste

2 tbsp water or milk

a dash of lemon juice, to taste

salt and pepper, to taste

Traditional, authentic hummus is made with tahini, a thick paste made from sesame seeds, which is uniquely bittersweet, both creamy and cloying, and can be difficult to come by in some supermarkets. I buy mine from a large independent grocer in town, but when I don't have it in, I use peanut butter in its place. It's not an exact match, but it's pretty close in a pinch.

First, drain your chickpeas in a sieve, and thoroughly rinse them under a cold tap to shake off the tinny taste they acquire from brining in their own ephemera. Tip the drained chickpeas into the large cup of a small bullet blender, or a food processor.

Peel the garlic and add to the chickpeas, along with the oil, peanut butter and water or milk. Pulse to a smooth, thick paste, adding a little more water or oil to reach your desired consistency, if needed.

Transfer the hummus to a bowl, scraping it carefully from the blender blades and sides of the cup to ensure you get every last precious drop. Season to taste with lemon juice, salt and pepper.

Store in the fridge in an airtight jar or container for up to 4 days.

Tuna Crunch Sandwich Spread

MAKES 1 DECENT-SIZED JAR

1 medium carrot

2 small pickled gherkins

1 pepper – any colour

1 tbsp any light vinegar

1 x 145g tin of tuna in brine or spring water

3 tbsp mayonnaise

1 tbsp tomato ketchup or tomato puree

½ tsp mustard – any kind

salt and pepper, to taste

This is based on the original Heinz sandwich spread that I loved throughout my childhood, with extra protein added to make it my own. Use it as a sandwich filler with fresh crunchy salad, or spread on crackers or toast, as a dip, or tossed through warm or cold pasta – it's very versatile and good for you. To make it vegan, use a vegan mayo and replace the tuna with roughly mashed cooked chickpeas.

First very finely chop your vegetables; it's easiest to do this by dicing them then pulsing briefly in a blender or food processor, but if you don't have one, grate the carrot and gherkins using the large holes on a box grater, and very finely chop the pepper by hand, taking care to discard the seeds and stalk.

Transfer the very small pieces of veg to a mixing bowl, and add the vinegar and salt and pepper.

Drain the tuna thoroughly in a sieve, giving it a quick rinse under a cold running tap to chase away any briny residue. Add it to the mixing bowl, and stir into the veg.

In a separate small bowl, combine your mayonnaise, ketchup or puree and mustard. Mix well until it is a uniform colour, then stir into the tuna and veg to coat it.

Spoon the sandwich spread into a clean jar, seal, and store in the fridge for up to 4 days. Not recommended for freezing.

Apple Peanut Butter V

MAKES 1 DECENT-SIZED JAR

2 large apples

2 tbsp honey

4 tbsp cold water

a dash of lemon juice

4 tbsp peanut butter (crunchy or smooth, whatever you prefer)

When I asked my readers for ideas for quick and easy snacks, several of them suggested apple wedges dunked in peanut butter. A fantastic idea, but the only apples I had in my fruit bowl at the time were soft and floral, rather than the crisp and slightly tart varieties I prefer, so I knocked them into this instead. Ideal for spreading on toast, crackers, bagels, plain biscuits like digestives or rich tea, or simply eating by the spoonful. To make it vegan, simply replace the honey with a liquid sweetener of your choice, like golden syrup or maple syrup.

Chop your apples into wedges and discard the core. Place the wedges into the small cup of a bullet blender, add the honey and a tablespoon or two of the water, with a dash of lemon juice to stop the apple from browning. Blend to a loose purée. Pour it into a small saucepan – a milk pan will do – and cook gently over a low heat for 10 minutes to thicken and reduce slightly.

Measure the peanut butter into a small bowl and add a tablespoon of the hot applesauce to the peanut butter. Mix well with a teaspoon to thin the peanut butter, then repeat, a tablespoon at a time, until all the applesauce is incorporated. Do not be tempted to rush this step – the beating in of the hot sauce to the peanut butter is essential; if you try to do it any faster, it may just end up a goopy mess.

Transfer to a clean jar, seal, and store in the fridge for up to 4 days. It may darken in colour slightly, this is normal, but do try to eat it as quickly as possible. I don't know what happens to it after 4 days – it's never lasted that long at my house!

Chicken Butter

MAKES 1 DECENT-SIZED JAR

6 chicken thighs, skin on

1 tbsp any light vinegar

6 tbsp mayonnaise

salt and pepper, to taste

There isn't actually any butter in this recipe, although you could add it if you liked, and it would surely only improve it in the way that butter improves almost everything (save for my arteries, but I made my peace with that some time ago now). But this is called chicken butter simply because it has the same texture, with a similar unctuous mouthfeel, and when thickly spread on bread or crackers, it's a very fine thing indeed, and a simple way to get a decent amount of protein without having to think about it too much. Chicken thighs are best here, because of the moist fat content and extra flavour they impart, but if you want a healthier option, chicken breasts would work.

First, heat your oven to 180°C/160°C fan/gas 4 and ensure there is a shelf just below the middle.

Place your chicken thighs, skin side up, in a small roasting tin. Season with a little salt and plenty of black pepper. Cook in the centre of the oven for 30 minutes. Remove, cover with tin foil, then cook for 20 minutes more.

Remove from the oven and allow to cool for 15 minutes, covered. Then strip the cooled chicken meat from the bones, including the skin, and place the chicken and skin in the large cup of a bullet blender, or in a food processor. Add all of the juices from the pan, using a rubber spatula to scrape it all out if needed – this is where the flavour is! (Keep the bones to make a stock, see Tip opposite.)

Add the vinegar and blend to a smooth paste. Measure in the mayonnaise, and blend again to combine. Spoon into a clean jar, seal, and store in the fridge. Use within 4 days.

TIPS

- *If you do use chicken breasts instead of chicken thighs, be sure to season generously as it might need a bit more help with flavour.*

- *I keep the leftover chicken bones to make a rich stock. I cover them in generously salted water in my slow cooker, along with a finely chopped carrot and onion and a little pinch of mixed dried herbs, and cook on high for an hour, then on low overnight. Strain it and use instead of water in the base for the Chicken Porridge (see page 136), or for soup, gravy or anything else you fancy.*

Cheese and Marmite Spread v

100g mayonnaise

2 tbsp Marmite or
similar yeast extract

30g hard strong
cheese

I keep a jar of this in my fridge door to dollop onto water crackers or fold through cold pasta for a quick, effortless snack, or to dip vegetables into when the mood takes me. It's simple, satisfyingly creamy and salty, and very very moreish.

Measure the mayonnaise into a small bowl, then spoon in the Marmite. Very finely grate the cheese into the bowl. Combine all three ingredients briskly and firmly with a sturdy fork; the Marmite will take some encouragement but persevere and it will come together just as you start to get exasperated with it.

Spoon it into a clean jar and screw the lid on tight. It will keep in the fridge for a week, but it rarely hangs around that long in my house.

Blue Cheese, Peanut Butter and Celery Leaf Pesto V

MAKES 1 SMALL
JAR, WHICH YIELDS
AROUND 6
PORTIONS

50g peanut butter
(crunchy or smooth,
whatever you prefer)

30g celery leaves

50g blue cheese
(any kind)

50g fresh parsley,
stalks and leaves

120ml light cooking
oil (olive if you're
fancy, rapeseed
or sunflower if
you're not)

30ml light vinegar
(red, white or cider
are fine)

Celery leaves are the big, flat, blousy leaves that adorn the sides of fresh celery crowns. Some supermarkets cut them off, which makes me wonder where on earth they end up, but most of the cheaper packages leave them intact. I use them as a salad leaf in their own right, to flavour cold jugs of water in summer, whizzed up with oil and salt and vinegar to make an all-purpose dressing, and sometimes in this rather lah-di-dah pesto. You can make it more of a dip by thinning it with natural yoghurt, or use it as it is as a spread for crackers or hot bagels, in a toasted sandwich, or tossed through hot or cold pasta with a bit of black pepper. It makes a fab dressing for a potato salad, tossed through warm cooked potatoes – tinned ones are absolutely fine in this instance.

Place the peanut butter into a small blender, along with the celery leaves, blue cheese and parsley, including any stalks. Pulse briefly for a few seconds at a time to blitz it all together. Add a dash of the oil if needed to loosen it – not all peanut butters, nor cheeses, are created equal.

Shake the blitzed leaves and nuts into a clean jar. Pour almost all the remaining oil into the cup of the blender and measure in the vinegar. Briefly blend to a smooth, creamy liquid, and pour it into the jar. Stir everything to coat, then top up with the last bit of oil to form a seal between the pesto and the top of the jar, which will help keep it fresher for longer.

Seal tightly and store in the fridge for up to 5 days, or the freezer for 3 months. Defrost thoroughly before using.

I file finger food firmly in the 'small and sophisticated' bracket in my mind. In reality, it's more like shoving carrot sticks and hummus in my face on a train from work event to work event, squished between the thighs of my fellow commuters who are glancing disdainfully at my noisy, smelly snack. Or Greek stuffed vine leaves, dripping all over my desk and keyboard, or an entire packet of Oreos eaten under the bedcovers and regretted for days afterwards as the crumbs prickle me in my sleep. But every louche restaurant these days seems to have an array of tiny morsels, designed to be shared with dining companions at the start or end of the meal. Mini desserts, sharing platters, amuse-bouches, palate cleansers; usually exorbitantly expensive and disappearing in the matter of a moment.

Finger food is mindless, it's easy, it's irreverent, it's portable and it doesn't require any pomp, circumstance, ceremony or cutlery. It can be eaten any time of day, between meals, to whet an appetite or fill a small hungry hole, on the go, al desko – whenever, wherever. I feel I have made a strong enough case for what is about to come now, so get stuck in. With both hands.

FINGER FOOD

Cheese and Oregano Rusks v

MAKES AROUND 12,
DEPENDING ON
SIZE OF COOKIE
CUTTER

250g self-raising flour, plus extra for dusting

30g hard strong cheese

½ tsp salt

1 tsp dried mixed herbs, or thyme or rosemary

120g butter, softened, plus extra for greasing

1 egg, beaten

1 tbsp full-fat milk

Rusks are one of the first foods that we give to weaning children; sturdy enough to be gripped in tiny grasping fists, but soft enough to suckle into a comforting nothingness. My taste for them as an adult never quite went away, and in times of despair, sadness or simply trawling the supermarket aisles looking for something simple to nibble on, I slip a box of Farley's rusks into my shopping basket, furtively burying them under the more respectable grown-up foods like bananas and vegetables. I sit in my kitchen with a cup of hot, sweet milky tea, dipping the edge in and sucking it gently, feeling immediately comforted and nourished and ever so slightly self-conscious. I hide them at the back of my cupboard, behind the sea salt crackers and respectable fare, but they are always there in times of need.

These rusks are based on an old English recipe, slightly less virtuous than their infant counterpart, with the addition of cheese and herbs. I include them here as a luxury version of a childhood classic, but if you'd rather nip to your nearest shop and pick up a box from the baby food aisle, I'm certainly in no position to judge you.

First heat your oven to 200°C/180°C fan/gas 6 and lightly grease a cookie sheet or baking tray. You may line it with greaseproof paper should you wish to, but it's not essential.

GOOD FOOD FOR BAD DAYS

Weigh the flour into a mixing bowl, finely grate in your cheese and stir in the salt and herbs. Spoon in the softened butter 1 teaspoon at a time, dotting it throughout the dry ingredients until it is all in the bowl. Rub the butter and salted flour together between your fingers until the flour resembles fine breadcrumbs, just as you would if you were making shortcrust pastry.

Beat together the egg and milk in a small bowl or measuring jug. Pour it into the centre of the mixing bowl and stir well to form a smooth, fairly dry but not crumbly, non-sticky dough. If your dough is tacky to the touch, simply add a tablespoon of flour and work it through, and repeat if required.

Lightly flour your worktop and tip the dough onto it. Roll it out evenly until it is around 2cm thick, then cut into rounds using a 5–8cm pastry cutter (they don't particularly have to be round now I come to think of it, but it ensures even cooking if they are all around the same size).

Carefully transfer each cutout piece of dough onto your baking tray, leaving a little space between them as they may spread and join together.

Bake for 10 minutes until risen and lightly coloured, then remove and allow to cool completely on the tray before attempting to transfer. Once cool, store in an airtight container, where they will keep for up to 4 days – if they last that long.

Orange and Blueberry Oat Bars V

200g porridge oats

160g dried
blueberries, raisins
or sultanas

100g sunflower seeds
or other seeds of
your choice

75g mixed peel
(optional)

180g marmalade

2 tbsp light cooking
oil, plus extra for
greasing

2 tbsp honey or
other liquid
sweetener of your
choice, to taste

You can use any dried fruit in place of the blueberries in these oat bars – I happen to like the tiny bursts of sweetness that semi-dried blueberries bring, but they aren't easy to find in every supermarket, so swap them out for sultanas, raisins, mixed peel or whatever takes your fancy. To make them vegan, simply switch the honey for golden syrup or another liquid sweetener of your choice.

First, heat your oven to 160°C/140°C fan/gas 3 and ensure there is a shelf just below the centre. Lightly grease a 20cm x 20cm baking tin or one of a similar size.

Weigh your porridge oats, blueberries or other fruit, seeds and mixed peel (if using) into a large mixing bowl. Mix well and set to one side for a moment.

Weigh the marmalade into a small, microwaveproof bowl and warm it on a high heat for 90 seconds. Stir carefully, then return to the microwave for a minute. Remove and stir well.

Pour the melted marmalade into the bowl of oats and fruit, and add the oil and honey or other sweetener. Mix well to incorporate, until all the oats are slightly sticky.

Pour the oats into the greased tin, pressing down firmly with the back of a spoon. Bake in the centre of the oven for 40 minutes. Remove and cool in the tin for 30 minutes to firm up, before cutting and serving.

These bars will keep in an airtight container for 3 days, or in the freezer for 3 months. Defrost thoroughly before serving.

Fennel and Pepper Oaties VE

MAKES AROUND 12

120g porridge oats

1 tbsp fennel seeds

a pinch of salt

1 tsp peppercorns

1 tbsp light cooking oil

2–4 tbsp warm water, as needed

a little plain flour, for dusting

If you don't have fennel seeds to hand, any aromatic spice seed will do – try caraway, poppy seeds, cardamom or cumin. They will each impart a completely different flavour, but they will be absolutely delicious regardless. These oaties are easily made gluten-free, simply swap the oats for a guaranteed gluten-free variety and use gluten-free flour. If you don't have gluten-free flour, simply sift the blended oats over the worktop briefly to lightly dust it, and use the remaining oats in the recipe.

Measure the oats, fennel, salt and peppercorns into the small cup of a bullet blender and pulse until finely ground to a breadcrumb consistency.

Pour the oats and spices into a large mixing bowl. Pour the oil and 2 tablespoons of the water into a small jar with a lid and screw the lid on tight. Shake vigorously to mix and emulsify, then pour over the oat mixture. Mix well to form a stiff but not crumbly dough. Add another tablespoon of water if needed, and another if needed after that. The dough should form balls when rolled in your fingers, but not fall apart or stick to your hands too much.

Chill the dough in the fridge for 30 minutes. Meanwhile, set your oven to 180°C/160°C fan/gas 4 and ensure there is a shelf just below the centre. Line or lightly grease a baking tray or cookie sheet and set to one side. Lightly flour your worktop and get your rolling pin out ready.

When the dough is chilled, gently roll it out to around 4mm thick. Cut into rounds and carefully place on your prepared baking tray. Squish the dough back together and roll out, until it's all used up.

Bake in the centre of the oven for 20 minutes, turning very carefully halfway through with a wide spatula to cook evenly. Remove from the oven and cool on the tray for a further 20 minutes to firm up, before moving them to an airtight container or freezer bag to store. Cool completely before sealing the container or bag. Will keep for 4 days, or 3 months in the freezer. Defrost completely and warm through in a low oven to serve.

Chocolate Cherry Oaty Bites VE

MAKES 12

2 ripe bananas

25g creamed coconut or butter

1–2 tbsp cocoa powder, to taste

120g porridge oats

75g semi-dried cherries

These take minutes to assemble and a few more minutes to cook. They also keep well, making them ideal nibbly snacks for when you know you should eat something, but what exactly that is evades you. Creamed coconut is the solid block found in the world food aisles, somewhere between coconut cream and coconut oil, but if you can't find it, butter or coconut oil will do just fine. These bites are pleasantly sweet without being overbearingly saccharine; what would be described as 'a guilt-free snack' in everyday parlance, but I gave up feeling guilty about eating a long while ago, so let's just dispense with the shame around certain foodstuffs and call them 'a snack'. You can find semi-dried or dried cherries in the baking aisle of most supermarkets, but glacé cherries or any dried fruit will do. Four of these constitutes two of your 5 a day, too, if you needed any further encouragement.

First, lightly grease a 12-cup fairy cake tin and set the oven to 160°C/140°C fan/gas 3 with a shelf just below the centre.

Peel your bananas, break them in half and pop them into the large cup of a bullet blender or food processor. Add the creamed coconut, or butter, the cocoa powder and 2 tablespoons of the oats. Blend to a thick paste and scrape every last drop into a mixing bowl.

Roughly chop the cherries and add to the bowl, along with the remaining oats. Mix well to coat all of the oats in the chocolate sauce mixture.

Divide the mixture between the cups of the cake tin and press down firmly with the back of a spoon. Bake for 12–15 minutes, then cool for a further 10 minutes in the tin before removing.

Will keep for 3 days in an airtight container if allowed to cool completely before transferring. Not recommended for freezing.

Peanut Butter, Honey and Marmite Popcorn v

SERVES 4.
ALLEGEDLY

2 tbsp peanut butter

1 tbsp butter or light cooking oil

2 tbsp honey

1 tsp Marmite

80g corn kernels

This came about by accident; I couldn't decide between peanut butter and Marmite popcorn, or peanut butter and honey, so on a whim I decided to amalgamate all three. And good lord, I have no regrets about it at all. The tang of Marmite, earthiness of the peanut butter and the sweet stickiness of the honey are a triumvirate of absolute bliss – my friend Caroline and I polished off the bowl faster than I could say, 'How many should this serve? Four? Oh. Us.' To make this vegan, replace the honey with golden syrup or another thick liquid sweetener of your choice.

First measure your peanut butter, butter or oil, honey and Marmite into a microwave-proof small bowl. Microwave on High for 45 seconds, until everything starts to melt. Remove carefully and stir vigorously to combine and melt any stubborn ingredients. Set to one side.

Grab a large nonstick pan with a lid and place it on the large hob ring over medium heat. Pour in the corn kernels – I like to spray the pan with Frylight or similar, but it doesn't need it, I'm just obsessed with keeping my pans unscathed as it's kind of my job. Pop the lid on and wait, jostling the pan every now and then to distribute the heat and prevent any kernels from burning in the hot spot.

When the corn starts to pop, shake the pan vigorously, keeping a good handle on the lid to stop it flying off and all the popcorn escaping! When the final 'pop' has popped, remove the pan from the heat, but leave the lid on for 5 more minutes, as some of the kernels take their time to wake up and realize their true potential – and babe, same.

When you're fairly confident that no popcorn is going to come flying out of the pan (I can tell you now, this confidence is misplaced, and 99% of the time a rogue piece of popcorn will make a bid for freedom), drench it in the sticky sauce and replace the lid, shaking vigorously to evenly coat it. Leave it to stand for a minute for the sauce to set, then tuck in while it's still warm.

Will keep for 2 days max in an airtight bag or container, but it's best eaten immediately.

As well as starting your day with a gentle self-congratulation for making it through to another morning, you should try to get something good inside you to set up your energy levels for whatever the day ahead will hold. If I forget to eat breakfast, I find myself lethargic, crabby and easily distracted – and it usually takes me a minute of confusion to work out why.

I always make sure my partner and child get a healthy, nutritious breakfast in the mornings, but between school runs and making packed lunches and all the other morning admin, sometimes I forget about myself in the process. I now keep a large jar of homemade granola in my eyeline and a pot of natural yoghurt in the fridge at all times, so if I do forget, I can dump a fistful of the former into the latter in a matter of seconds, take it to my desk, and get on with my day.

BREAKFAST & BRUNCH

Breakfast Bowl v

SERVES 1

2 scoops (4 level tbsp)
vanilla protein shake

2 tbsp porridge oats

100g frozen fruit

250ml milk or half
milk and half water

4 tbsp granola (see
page 75) or cereal of
your choice

fresh fruit, to serve

I make a variation on this breakfast bowl a couple of times a week, sometimes for Small Boy, but mostly for Mrs J, who is an avid cyclist, clocking up around 500 miles a month. The protein shake is really the point of it, for muscle repair and recovery, and the rest just makes it enjoyable rather than something to endure. If you don't have any protein shake to hand, however, add an extra 2 tablespoons of oats, as they are also a reasonable source of protein, but you'll need to add more milk or water, as the smoothie will be incredibly thick.

I vary the fruit depending on what we have in, and I am yet to find a combination that doesn't work. Frozen is best for an instantly cold, soft ice-cream consistency, but tinned and fresh will do in a pinch. Sometimes I get fancy and spray the fruit with edible glitter, or add a rice-paper kitten, or cut the fruit into little star shapes, but these bowls are just as delicious without all the frippery.

Measure the protein shake and oats into the large cup of a bullet blender, or the jug of a standard blender. Add the fruit and cover with the milk, or half milk and half water. Blend to a smooth, thick consistency, 40ish seconds at a time. Do not run the blender continuously, as it can burn out the motor.

Pour the smoothie into a large bowl – a pasta bowl is ideal. Scatter the granola or cereal over the top, and add fruit to serve.

GOOD FOOD FOR BAD DAYS

Will keep in the fridge for 24 hours, covered, but tastes best when made fresh. If the smoothie splits or separates in the fridge, as some fruits are liable to do, just give it a brisk stir to bring it back together, and enjoy.

'Like eating a bowl of love ... Of all the things you make me, I look forward to these the most.' - Mrs J.

Carrot Cake Baked Oats V

SERVES 2

2 small apples

2 medium carrots

400ml vanilla milk (soya or dairy, see intro)

80g sultanas or raisins

100g porridge oats

¼ tsp ground cinnamon

a dash of grated nutmeg

cold milk or natural yoghurt, to serve

I use ready-made vanilla soya milk for these, making this recipe vegan, but if you like you can use standard milk and a dash of vanilla. The vanilla is really optional, as it's expensive, but it does add that extra sumptuous note of comfort. These oats make for a hearty but healthy breakfast or a delicious dessert, loading you up with three of your 5 a day.

First heat your oven to 180°C/160°C fan/gas 4, and place a shelf just below the centre, if it isn't there already.

Next, core and dice the apples and one of the carrots, then pop them in a bullet blender, or the jug of a standard blender or food processor. Pour over the milk and blend until smooth and a delightful pale-peachy colour.

Pour the liquid into a large mixing bowl. Grate in the remaining carrot, and measure in the sultanas or raisins and oats. Add the cinnamon and nutmeg, then stir well to evenly distribute the ingredients throughout the mixture.

Bake in the centre of the oven for 35–40 minutes, or until softly firm throughout.

Serve immediately, with cold milk or natural yoghurt – whatever takes your fancy. Will keep in the fridge in a sealed container for 2 days. Heat through completely to serve.

Peanut, Honey and Apple Overnight Oats V

MAKES 2 SIZEABLE PORTIONS

100g porridge oats

¼ tsp ground cinnamon

2 apples, cored and cut in half

250ml honey nut milk (see page 30), plus extra to serve

honey, to taste

natural yoghurt, to serve

Overnight oats, sometimes known as Bircher porridge, are a love letter to your tomorrow self. They take a moment to prepare, but in that moment, you're investing in your own health and wellbeing for the day that will follow. You're taking care of yourself, setting yourself up for a good day. I cobble together Bircher with whatever fruit is on the turn in the fridge of an evening, and the next morning I'm always super grateful that it's ended up in there and not in the bin. A perfectly portable snack for commuting to work, or eating al desko, or just enjoying in a quiet moment, or grabbing spoonfuls of it between school runs, or however you have it. It's a healthy start to the day, with oats, protein, slow-release carbohydrates and plenty of fruit to get you going.

Measure your oats into a large mixing bowl, add the cinnamon, and grate in the apples. Mix well, and quickly, to protect the apples from browning.

Pour over the honey nut milk, and stir until well combined.

Transfer the mixture to an airtight container and rest in the fridge for 8 hours, or overnight.

Serve with honey, to taste, and a splash more milk or a dollop of natural yoghurt.

Will keep for 2 days in the fridge in an airtight container. Stir well before serving, and loosen with additional milk as required. Not recommended for freezing.

Raspberry Bakewell Baked Oats VE

SERVES 2-4

1 tbsp oil, for greasing the tin

80g porridge oats

160g fresh or frozen raspberries, allowed to defrost

375ml almond milk

a drop or two of vanilla essence (optional)

flaked almonds (optional)

These baked oats take mere seconds to throw together and taste like a dessert. Ideal for any time of day, but a brilliant way to set yourself up for the day ahead with a small, decadent act of care, reminiscent of lunchbox treats and school trips. If you don't have any almond milk to hand, any milk will do. Full-fat is best, but you can use whatever you fancy.

First heat your oven to 180°C/160°C fan/gas 4, and place a shelf just below the centre. Lightly grease a small roasting tin or loaf tin with the lightest of touches; a pastry brush dipped in oil will suffice, it's just to stop the oats from sticking to the sides too much.

Measure the oats and raspberries into the tin, and pour over the milk. Add the vanilla essence, if using, and stir briefly to combine. Top with the flaked almonds, if you have them.

Bake in the centre of the oven for 30–35 minutes, until the oats have absorbed all of the milk and are soft and swollen.

Remove from the oven, and enjoy.

These baked oats are delicious straight from the oven, on their own, or smashed up in a bowl with cold milk poured over the top. You can also bake them for 5–10 minutes longer until they resemble a soft flapjack, allow them to cool completely, and slice into fingers for simple, good snacks.

They will keep for 2 days in the fridge in an airtight container, and they reheat well in the oven.

Fluffernut French Toast v

SERVES 1, HEARTILY

1 egg

a splash of milk

1 tbsp sugar, honey, or other sweetener of choice

a few pinches of cinnamon

2 thick slices of white bread

2 tbsp peanut butter

2 big marshmallows

1 tbsp sugar, optional

butter/oil, to fry

This abominable pile of sugar is a very very rare treat in our household, and it wouldn't have existed at all were it not for my hapless disorganization and reckless parenting style. It was Monday 14 October, the day this book was due to be handed to my editor and publisher to review the first draft. I had been at my desk overnight until 5am, then I snuck away for an hour's nap and was back in my chair just after 6. Sometime around 8am, my Small Boy appeared, bleary eyed in mismatched pyjamas. And I realized we were running late, I hadn't been grocery shopping, and he needed some breakfast, pronto. I panicked and grabbed a white bread roll, carefully cut some of the crust away, basted it in the last beaten egg and fried it in the pan. We were out of beans, plum tomatoes, and I'd just used my last egg. 'Sod it', I thought, and started pulling things out of the baking cupboard to top it with. Small Boy was delighted. I then put extra veg in his lunchbox to assuage my pangs of parental guilt as he crammed this toast into his face.

Crack the egg into a small bowl, and whisk in the milk, sugar and cinnamon until well combined. Slice your bread diagonally down the middle to create four equal-sized pieces, and dip each one in the egg mixture, then set to one side. If you don't mind the slightly extra washing up, I place my bread pieces in a small roasting tin, packed tight, and then pour the egg mix over the top to make sure they are evenly coated, but I understand entirely if this is a fanny too far for anyone else. Regardless, coat your bread in the eggy mix.

Gently warm a nonstick pan on a medium heat, and add the oil. Place a few pieces of bread in and fry for 3 minutes on each side, until they are crisp and golden. You may need to do these in batches, so have a plate handy to place them on, or a clean worktop.

When the French toasts are all cooked, spread half of them with peanut butter, and dollop a large marshmallow in the centre, or a scattering of small ones. Place a plain piece of bread on top, like making a sandwich, and return to the pan on a low heat for 2 minutes to melt the marshmallow and peanut butter together. Serve immediately!

Microwave Lemon Curd and Blueberry Porridge v

SERVES 1

80g frozen or fresh blueberries, or other fruit

250ml milk or half milk and half water

40g porridge oats

1 generous tbsp lemon curd

I always keep a jar of lemon curd on hand; it's an easy storecupboard staple for adding sweetness and zing to a multitude of meals, from simple fried rice to folding through vanilla soft-scoop ice cream, it's one of my most favourite things. This can be made in minutes, and it's like starting your day with a cuddle, taking five minutes to yourself to just linger in a moment of bliss. Or just bolt the lot in one sitting and go back to bed, safe in the knowledge that you've had at least one of your 5 a day and some slow-release energy to tide you over for a bit. If you don't have any blueberries on hand, almost any fresh, canned or frozen fruit will do: blackberries, cherries, sliced tinned pears, peaches – probably not grapefruit because the acidity may split the porridge. But now I've said that, contrary as I am, I'm tempted to give it a go ...

Instructions for an 800W microwave:

First choose your bowl – this makes a hearty amount, so you'll want something of a reasonable size with a bit of depth to it. And make sure it is microwave-safe – so no metal on the rim or anything like that.

Place your blueberries, or other fruit, in the bottom of the bowl. Pour over the milk or half milk and half water and measure in the oats, then dollop the lemon curd in the centre. Cover with cling film and make a small hole in the centre to ventilate. If you don't want to use cling film, balance a plate on top that covers the bowl completely.

GOOD FOOD FOR BAD DAYS

Microwave on full power for 2 minutes. Remove carefully, and take off the cover. Stir briskly to combine, and leave to stand for 60 seconds. Cover, then return to the microwave for 60 seconds longer. Remove, stir thoroughly to eliminate any hot spots, and leave to stand for a minute more, before enjoying.

Will keep in the fridge for 24 hours in an airtight jar or container, but it is likely to thicken as it cools, so thin with a little extra milk before storing. Heat through completely in the microwave to serve, or enjoy as a Bircher-style cold breakfast by adding a few tablespoons of natural yoghurt.

Banana Sultana Bread VE

**MAKES 1 SMALL
LOAF**

4 bananas (around
320g)

80ml cooking oil,
plus extra for
greasing

225g self-raising flour

2 tsp baking powder

2 tsp ground
cinnamon

120g raisins or
sultanas

*This recipe is an adaptation of the original Vegan Banana
Bread from A Girl Called Jack, only with the fruit
bolstered up to provide two portions of our 5 a day per
two slices of it (one portion of banana and one of
sultanas). I don't add any extra sugar to this recipe as the
sweetness of the bananas and sultanas is enough – and it
is on the heavy side, like a middling Christmas pudding
weight, rather than a light sponge.*

Preheat your oven to 180°C/160°C fan/gas 4, and place a shelf just
below the centre, then lightly grease a 450g loaf tin.

Peel and mash the bananas with the cooking oil in a mixing bowl
– it will look a bit horrendous at this stage and it takes a little
work, so if you have a small personal blender or bullet blender,
it's easier to just pop them in that along with the oil and blast it
to a smooth puree, then pour into a bowl.

Stir the flour, baking powder and cinnamon into the bananas,
and mix well to form a batter. Fold in the raisins or sultanas to
distribute them evenly, breaking them up if they have stuck
together in the bag.

Pour the batter into the prepared loaf tin and bake for 45 minutes
in the centre of the oven, until the loaf is risen and golden. If a
knife or skewer inserted into the middle comes out clean, it's
done. If it's a little sticky, give it 10 more minutes, then try again.

Remove from the oven and allow the bread to cool in the tin for
30 minutes to firm up, before turning out and slicing.

This will keep, well wrapped, for up to 4 days.

Jalapeno Cheese Scones V

**MAKES AROUND 10,
DEPENDING ON
THE SIZE YOU
PREFER**

100g mature
Cheddar cheese

2 tbsp pickled
jalapenos from a jar,
drained

125g full-fat cream
cheese

4 tbsp milk or water

4 tbsp light cooking
oil

2 eggs

1 tbsp baking powder

a pinch of salt and
black pepper

240g plain flour, plus
extra for dusting

*These fiery little scones require just a few minutes' work
before they're popped in the oven – ideal for breakfast,
brunch, lunch, or any time of day. I like mine with a
poached egg for breakfast, and I've heard a rumour that
it's pretty good stuffed with crispy bacon, too.*

Finely grate your Cheddar cheese and very finely chop your
jalapenos. Combine in a small bowl and set to one side.

Measure the cream cheese into a large mixing bowl, then add the
milk or water, oil and one of your eggs. Beat thoroughly until
they combine into a uniform mixture. Add your baking powder,
salt and pepper, cheese and jalapenos, and mix again.

Add the flour 2 tablespoons at a time, first to form a batter, then
gradually to make a soft, even, pliable dough.

Heavily flour your work surface and tip the dough onto it. Knead
lightly for 2–3 minutes to bring it all together.

Heat your oven to 200°C/180°C fan/gas 6, and set a shelf just below
the middle. Line a baking tray with greaseproof paper.

Roll out your dough to around 4cm thick, and cut into rounds
with a 7cm cookie cutter. Place each round carefully on the
baking tray, leaving 3cm clear around each one. Repeat until all
your dough is used up. Beat the remaining egg in a small bowl or
cup, and brush onto each scone liberally.

Bake for 12 minutes in the centre of the oven, until risen and
golden. Remove and allow to cool for 10 minutes before serving.
They will keep for 3 days in an airtight container or 3 months in
the freezer.

GOOD FOOD FOR BAD DAYS

Cinnamon Seed Granola VE

SERVES 4ISH

160g porridge oats

2 tbsp sunflower seeds

2 tbsp golden linseed (optional)

1 tbsp oil, or generous amount of spray oil if you prefer

1 tsp ground cinnamon

a pinch of salt

2 tbsp golden syrup or honey

This quick granola is delicious warm, eaten straight from the pan, or cool and chunky, with ice-cold milk. I serve it on top of ice cream, on yoghurt in granola pots on the go, or just eat it by the handful. The seeds can be swapped out for any that take your fancy or that you have in.

Measure the oats, sunflower seeds and linseed into a large, nonstick pan. Drizzle over the oil, if using, or spray Frylight or similar, if you'd rather. Add the cinnamon and a pinch of salt.

Cook over medium heat for 10 minutes, until the oats start to toast slightly. Stir intermittently to cook evenly and stop them from sticking and burning.

Drizzle the syrup or honey over, and turn the heat up to high. Stir continuously for 1 minute until the oats start to clump together, then remove from the heat and cool completely.

Store in a clean, sealed airtight jar or container for 3 weeks.

Bounty Brek v

MAKES 6-8
PORTIONS

250g porridge oats

50g coconut milk
powder

3 tbsp cocoa powder

2 tbsp sugar or
sweetener, as
preferred

milk, to serve

A bastardization of two of my favourite things from childhood, Ready Brek and Bounty bars, amalgamated into one swift breakfast that takes just three minutes to make. If you really feel like cheating, you can just ping the kettle on and make it in a mug, because sometimes that's exactly what's needed.

Measure your oats into the large cup of a bullet blender, or the jug of a standard blender or food processor. Pulse for 10 seconds at a time so as not to overwork the motor, until the oats are finely ground – not as finely as flour, you want more of a sawdust consistency.

Transfer the ground oats to a large airtight jar. Measure in the coconut milk powder, cocoa powder and sugar or sweetener. Replace the lid and shake well to evenly distribute.

To use, add 50g (just shy of half a cup) of the cereal mix to 250ml boiling water and stir well. Leave to stand for 3 minutes, then stir in a splash of milk to your desired consistency, and enjoy.

Big Baked Banana Pancake v

SERVES 2, GENEROUSLY

1 tbsp oil, for greasing the tin

2 large ripe bananas

200ml full-fat milk

175g self-raising flour

1 tsp baking powder

½ tsp ground cinnamon

We love pancakes in my little household and we have them frequently, but when I'm on my own on a rare weekend morning, it seems a bit of a palaver to make them just for myself. As much as I love them, I just can't be bothered to babysit them ten seconds at a time. This oven-baked version is a perfect compromise, to fling in the oven and forget about. Cooking this big pancake this way means it rises brilliantly, so you get more pancake for less effort, and that's something I can definitely get on board with. It's easy to upscale to feed a crowd, or slice it into wedges like a pizza, stack it up, and slather it in butter, syrup, or a pile of berries with a light dusting of icing sugar.

First set your oven to 180°C/160°C fan/gas 4 and lightly grease a 20cm round cake tin, making sure to get right into the edges and up the sides. Pop it in the oven to heat the tin and oil for the best results.

Quickly – so your oil doesn't start to smoke – peel your bananas and pop them in the large cup of your bullet blender, or the jug of a standard blender. Add the milk, flour, baking powder and cinnamon, and blend to a smooth batter.

Carefully remove the tin from the oven, and pour in the batter, scraping out the jug with a plastic spatula or spoon to get every last delicious drop. Return the tin to the oven and bake for 15 minutes, until risen and golden.

CONTINUES OVER THE PAGE →

Remove from the oven and allow the pancake to cool for a couple of minutes, so it firms up slightly, else it might fall apart when you try to remove it! Run a knife around the edge to release any sticky bits, and gently lift out of the tin.

The cooked pancake will keep in the fridge for 2 days, wrapped or stored in an airtight container, but it is best eaten immediately. Warm through to serve – 90 seconds in the microwave ought to do it. Serve with butter, jam, syrup or a pile of fresh berries.

Slow-Cooker Bread VE

IN A 1.3 LITRE SLOW
COOKER:

260g plain flour
(after many years
of obstinacy I will
concur that bread
flour is better, but
bog-standard plain
flour does work),
plus extra for
dusting

7g dried active yeast

a pinch of salt

260ml warm water

a little oil, for
greasing

Each compartment of my triple slow cooker is 1.3 litres, so to make matters simple, and after a little trial and error, I worked out that the optimum amount of flour to make a loaf of really good bread in it is 260g. I started at 350g, and upon seeing how splendidly it rose, reduced it down – my first attempt ended up with dough stuck to the lid of the cooker, trying fervently to escape! If your slow cooker is larger than mine, you can pop the dough in a loaf tin.

This bread does not need to rise or prove as it does all that in the slow cooker, but for best results, when you turn your cooker on for 20 minutes to preheat, you can leave the dough to rise a little to give it a headstart.

You will also need baking or greaseproof paper, for the best results.

Now with all that in mind, let's make the simplest, softest bread you've ever made! Once you have the hang of it, you can add all sorts to it – I have made mine with beer, coconut milk, orange juice, beetroot juice, spinach and an array of herbs and spices, but before we play around too much, it's important to crack the basics.

Grab a large mixing bowl, and weigh in the flour carefully. Add the yeast and salt and mix well to combine.

Make a well – a sort of hole – in the centre and add most of the water. Using a blunt knife (like a butter, palette or standard dinner knife), mix the flour and liquid together, starting from the

CONTINUES OVER THE PAGE →

wet middle and working it out to the dry edges, to form a dough. You may find you do not need all of the liquid – not all flours are created equal.

Heavily flour your worktop – a third of a cup of flour or a generous handful – and tip the dough onto it. Lightly oil your hands – this will stop the dough from sticking to them, and incorporating a little fat into your bread baking also helps the crumb structure to form or some science like that. It's a good thing, anyway. Knead the dough for a few minutes – common wisdom suggests 10 minutes, but you will need strong shoulders to pull this off, so 3 or 4 will do if you put your back into it. To knead, I find it best to visualize an assailant; if that kind of thing doesn't trigger you, or if it does, I'm very sorry, this is just what works for me. First, drive your palm into the dough and push it away from you like a mugger trying to nick your mobile phone on a dark night. POW! Grab it by the scruff of the neck at the back and pull it back towards you. Flip it over. Throw it down. Whack it again. BAM! This should feel satisfying and slightly bizarre. Repeat, putting your back into it, really driving the force of your forearm and shoulder into it, until you feel it start to spring to life beneath your hands. If it starts to stick, add a tad more flour.

Set to one side for 20 minutes to relax a little after you've duffed it about a bit. You both kinda need a rest now.

Lightly grease a piece of greaseproof paper big enough to line your slow cooker pot with the edges poking out, then pop it in – it doesn't have to be neat, the bread will see to that as it expands. Drop the dough in on top of the paper, pop the lid on, and set a timer for an hour and 30 minutes. Walk away.

Then, 90 minutes later, go back to your bread. Gently gently remove it from the slow cooker. Peel away the greaseproof paper and turn the bread over, so the odd-looking undercooked side is now on the bottom. Pop it back in for the remaining 40 minutes.

When the time is up, remove the bread from the slow cooker and give it a tap on the top. It should feel light and sound hollow, if it doesn't, pop it back in for 20 more minutes. The steam/heat trapped in the slow cooker means that it won't dry out the way that conventional bread does in the oven, in fact, you should notice that it is a lot softer and squidgier than crusty oven-baked bread, and that to me is part of its appeal.

When well and truly done, remove from the cooker, allow to cool on a wire rack for 20 minutes, then slice and enjoy.

This bread will keep, well wrapped, for 3 days in a cool dry place. It can be frozen for up to 3 months, then toasted from frozen.

It may seem an alarming admission for a cookery author, but sometimes wrangling with the mere thought of having to cook a meal for myself from scratch on a bad day, or when I have little spare energy, is just too much. I usually spend more time trying to wheedle myself into the kitchen than it would take to prepare a quick dinner in the first place!

Cheese toasties and jazzed-up Pot Noodles to one side, these are my favourite speedy suppers for getting something on the table or inside my tummy without trashing the entire kitchen or creating a mountain of washing up.

FIFTEEN MINUTES OR LESS

Cacio e Pepe v

SERVES 1

½ tsp salt

100g spaghetti

butter, to taste

plenty of hard strong
cheese, to taste

cracked black
pepper, to taste

I first had cacio e pepe in Venice – on a 48-hour bolt away on a whim with my friend Russell, to blast away a creeping depression that was starting to overwhelm me. The trip was impulsive; he was there already and I needed to run away from my four walls for a moment or two, to wander, to eat with abandon, to explore and enjoy. We wandered through cobbled streets, drank Negronis with chilli-stuffed fat olives in bars, stayed out until the small hours and ate pasta several times a day. It was in these short 48 hours that I had my first risi e bisi and cacio e pepe, and I associate both with the comfort of being listened to, the wonder of new adventures and the gentle shoulders-down, opulent contentment of the company of an old friend. Cacio e pepe is simple, but not austere. Easy, but the rewards for such little effort are abundant in their dividends. It is simply pasta, butter, cheese and pepper; once you master this recipe, you're only ever eight minutes from gratifying satiation. Which is quicker, and far cheaper, than a flight to Venice.

Bring a medium saucepan of water to the boil and salt it generously. Drop your pasta into it and stir once or twice to shift any pieces that might be thinking about settling on the bottom of the pan. Cover the pan and reduce to a simmer for 8–10 minutes, depending on your pasta.

Meanwhile, dice your butter into cubes if it is firm, or scoop up a large spoonful if it is soft. Set to one side. Grate your cheese very finely – plenty of it.

When the pasta is soft – and I like this particular dish nursery-soft – drain and quickly return to the pan. Add the butter, most of the cheese and a few generous grinds of black pepper. Serve topped with yet more cheese and pepper.

This does not keep brilliantly – although saying that, cold and slightly stiff cacio e pepe is still preferable to having none at all. If you're willing to accept a below-par version, you can chill it in the fridge for up to 24 hours. Reheat thoroughly in a pan to serve and loosen with more butter. Absolutely not recommended for freezing.

Lingreenie V

a few pinches of salt

100g spaghetti or linguine

80g spinach or kale

40g spring onions

80g green courgettes or more

1 tbsp any oil

1 tbsp lemon juice

finely grated favourite cheese, to serve

plenty of black pepper or a few chilli flakes

Eating your greens needn't be a chore – here I combine two and a half of your recommended 5 a day with a bowl of buttery, comforting pasta. I make this for myself when I'm in a funk and know I need something good but don't have the time nor the energy to really think about what. For extra comfort, just up the butter and cheese!

Fill a medium saucepan two-thirds full with water and salt it generously. Bring to the boil, then snap your spaghetti or linguine in half and pop it in. You can stick half in and wait for it to soften before nudging in the other half, which is the traditional method, but most of the time I just do this instead, as it's less effort. Reduce the pan to a simmer and cover with a lid, if you have one, or a sturdy plate, if you don't. This retains the heat, meaning it cooks faster and is more energy-efficient.

Meanwhile, stuff the spinach or kale into the large cup of a bullet blender, followed by the spring onions. Roughly dice your courgettes and add that too. Add the oil and lemon juice and pulse to a smooth, bright green paste. Set to one side. (See below for how to make it without a blender.)

When the pasta is cooked – around 8 minutes if covered, 10 minutes if not – drain most of the salty water away, reserving a little. Add a splash of the reserved cooking water to the green sauce to loosen it slightly and bring out the bright flavours. Return the pasta to the pan and pour over the sauce. Toss briefly until well coated, and finish with finely grated cheese and black pepper or chilli flakes. Serve hot, immediately, or enjoy chilled from the fridge – both work well!

TIP

- *If you don't have a blender, you can still make this recipe – it won't be a smooth, pesto-style sauce, but it will still be delicious:*

  Finely chop your spinach or kale by hand – the easiest way to do this is to roll it tightly into a sausage shape and slice thinly with a heavy flat knife. Pop it in a bowl. Mince your spring onion by finely slicing it then chopping it vigorously to smithereens. Grate your courgette. Mix everything together with the oil and lemon juice and season with plenty of black pepper. And think about investing in a bullet blender, if you can, as they are a go-to for simple, fuss-free meals in a hurry!

Anchovy Butter Pasta

SERVES 2, WITH LEFTOVER BUTTER

100g butter

1 x 90g tin or jar of anchovies

120g spaghetti or linguine

1 x 400g tin of green or brown lentils

1 large courgette

plenty of black pepper

a dash of lemon juice

I first made anchovy butter in my kitchen at home on the cusp of autumn 2019. Faced with a pile of courgettes to use and a recipe book to write, I began to throw together whatever I had to hand to turn the pile of fat green vegetables in my fridge drawer into delicious dishes. It was 2pm, and I was trying to wrap up soon so I could pick my son up from school. I wanted something super quick, simple and that would keep for my dinner that evening. I poured a tin of anchovies in the blender, along with all of the oil, and added butter, on a whim. I pulsed it, watching the butter whip to a cupcake frosting consistency, flecked with freckles of brown. I gently braced myself as I dipped a tentative finger in. The smell was overpowering – I closed my eyes and sucked that finger and I swear my ovaries and arteries both gave the same deep internal groan – one in pleasure, one in fear. This is how I will die, I thought to myself. Spooning anchovy butter from my blender until my heart packs in. Like Elvis Presley, but with a touch more dignity, and a faint aroma of the sea.

Friends, this anchovy butter is phenomenal. For my vegetarian readers, you could substitute anchovies for Henderson's relish, if you're still reading this far. And it didn't keep for dinner. I ran all the way to school, late, because I devoured the entire pan meant for two with no regrets at all.

First pop your butter into the small cup of a bullet blender and tip the anchovies over the top, making sure to include any oil from the tin or jar. Pulse until well combined, then transfer to a clean jar with a lid until needed.

Bring a large saucepan of water to the boil and feed in the spaghetti or linguine gently, pushing it in as the submerged ends start to soften, until it all collapses into the boiling pan. If you're in a hurry, you can snap it in half and sling the lot in, but on occasion I find something quite soothing about standing watching spaghetti soften.

Drain and rinse the lentils and tip them into the pan a moment after the pasta. Reduce to a simmer and cook for 8–10 minutes until the pasta is cooked.

While the pasta cooks, grate your courgette using the fat holes on the side of a box grater or a julienne peeler, if you have one. Set to one side with the anchovy butter – you'll need both in a moment.

When the spaghetti is cooked and the lentils are soft, drain both together then return them to the pan. Add the courgette to wilt in the residual heat of the spaghetti, then add the anchovy butter a tablespoon at a time, to taste. I like 4 tablespoons between two people, but I am a glutton for salt and fat, and you may not be.

Finish with plenty of black pepper and a dash of lemon juice to brighten those deep intense flavours, and serve piping hot.

Will keep in the fridge for 2 days; reheat until piping hot to serve. The leftover butter will also keep in a clean jar for up to 4 days. Not recommended for freezing.

Triple Tomato Soup VE

SERVES 2

1 x 400g tin of tomato soup

1 x 400g tin of chopped tomatoes

100g sundried tomatoes in oil

1 tbsp balsamic vinegar

salt and pepper, to taste

This recipe is so simple that it feels audacious even calling it a recipe at all, but here we are. It's one of those that is so much more than the sum of its parts and takes mere seconds to throw together. I have made it for friends in a hurry, realizing that they are present for a mealtime and I haven't prepared anything, and they all invariably adore it. It also makes an excellent pasta sauce or a base for something more fancy; feel free to pad it out with beans or legumes, vegetables, a slosh of fancy vinegar, pesto or herb oil as you see fit.

Open the tin of tomato soup and pour it carefully into the large cup of your bullet blender or the jug of a standard blender. Add the chopped tomatoes and the sundried tomatoes, with a little of their oil. Slosh in the vinegar and blend everything together in bursts until completely smooth. The sundried tomatoes may take some work, but they'll get there.

Pour the contents of the blender into a medium, heavy-bottomed saucepan over a medium hob ring. Heat gently for 10 minutes, stirring intermittently. Season to taste with salt and pepper, and serve.

I like to freeze half of this in a Tupperware container before cooking it, so I always have some to hand. You can heat it from frozen in the microwave, cooking for 4 minutes on High, then removing to stir, and returning it for 3 more minutes. Handy to have in a hurry, for very little effort at all.

GOOD FOOD FOR BAD DAYS

One-Pan Cheesesteak Pasta

SERVES 2, GENEROUSLY

160g wholegrain pasta

120g onion or frozen diced onions

140g mixed peppers or frozen sliced

140g fresh mushrooms or frozen sliced

200ml milk

100g mature Cheddar cheese

plenty of black pepper

½ tsp dried mixed herbs

1 x 500g tin of stewed steak

This recipe will make two very generous portions, each of which contains three of your 5 a day. Not bad for less than fifteen minutes' work.

First, bring a pan of salted water to the boil and pour in the pasta, onions, peppers and mushrooms. Reduce to a simmer and cook for 8 minutes, until the pasta is al dente.

Drain any excess water, then return the pasta to the pan and add the milk. Grate in the cheese and stir well through the hot pasta. Season well with plenty of black pepper and the herbs.

Drain the stewed steak into a fine-mesh sieve and run under cold water for a minute, jiggling it slightly to get as much of the gravy off as possible. Tip the meat into the pan and stir into the pasta. Cover and cook over low heat for 5 more minutes, for the pasta to finish cooking and the cheese to melt.

Serve hot or cold. Will keep in the fridge for 3 days, or frozen for 3 months. Defrost completely before reheating.

Quick and Spicy Salmon Noodles

SERVES 1 HUNGRY
PERSON WITH
LEFTOVERS

100g onion or frozen
sliced onions

1 tbsp fresh root
ginger, grated

1 clove of garlic,
grated

400ml full-fat
coconut milk

1 stock cube

1 tbsp curry powder

a pinch of chilli, to
taste

black pepper, to taste

1 x 170g tin of salmon
or jar of salmon
paste

100g dried noodles

70g frozen edamame
beans or peas

a dash of lime or
lemon juice

*These noodles take mere minutes to throw together, and
you can pad them out with veg to make them go further
and ramp up their nutritional value – I sometimes like to
add a cupful of those small, diced, mixed frozen
vegetables and some extra peas, too. Don't be put off by
the jar of salmon paste suggestion; I've found it to be a
surprisingly versatile ingredient in speedy budget cookery,
and it works well here.*

Measure your onion into a large, heavy-bottomed saucepan. Add
the ginger and garlic, and pour over the coconut milk. Crumble
in the stock cube and add the curry powder, chilli and pepper.
Bring to the boil, then reduce to a simmer. Drain the salmon
and tip into the saucepan, or stir in the salmon paste. Stir well
to combine, then cover and cook on a vigorous simmer for
4 minutes.

Add the noodles and the edamame or peas and replace the lid.
Continue to cook for 6 minutes at a slightly less vigorous simmer,
then turn off the heat. Allow to stand for a few minutes for the
sauce to thicken as it cools and the noodles continue to cook in
the residual steam.

Serve with a dash of lemon or lime juice and extra black pepper,
to taste.

Green Minestrone v

SERVES 2 VERY GENEROUSLY, OR 4 AS A LIGHT MEAL

120g frozen diced onions

50g small pasta

1 x 400g tin of cannellini or haricot beans

a generous fistful of fresh parsley, basil or a mix of both

1 tbsp garlic paste

1 chicken or vegetable stock cube or bouillon powder

120g frozen spinach or kale

50g cheese, any kind you please

120g frozen peas

1–2 tsp lemon juice, to taste

black pepper, to taste

At my fastest, I have whipped this up in eight minutes from start to finish with a freshly boiled kettle, but it usually takes around ten without some degree of organization. You'll need the smallest pasta you can find – I use the tiny stars, which are sometimes in the baby food aisle of the supermarket instead of with the regular-sized pasta. Like most recipes, this benefits from being allowed to cool and rest for a while after cooking, but it's fine to eat straight away if you're in a hurry.

Fill your kettle and pop it on to boil.

Measure the onion and pasta into a large nonstick pan, preferably one with a lid. Drain the beans and add them to the pan. Finely chop the parsley or basil and scatter in, along with the garlic paste. By this time, your kettle should have boiled.

Pour in 450ml boiling water and add the stock cube or bouillon powder. Drop in the frozen spinach or kale, grate in the cheese and add the peas. Stir everything well, before covering the pan with a lid. Set it on high heat on your largest hob ring for a minute, then reduce to medium heat and a vigorous simmer. Keep an eye on it, it will take 7–8 minutes for the pasta to cook.

Stir intermittently every couple of minutes to break up the spinach and mix everything together. When the pasta and veg are cooked, remove from the heat and add lemon juice and pepper to taste. Stir well, and serve.

Will keep in the fridge for up to 3 days, cooled and stored in a clean airtight jar or container. Can be frozen for up to 3 months; defrost completely in the fridge before heating through to serve.

Five-a-Day Couscous VE

120g frozen diced onion

100g frozen sliced peppers

1 medium carrot

1 tbsp light cooking oil

1 x 400g tin of chickpeas

60g sultanas or raisins

120g dried couscous

400ml chicken or veg stock

a few handfuls of spinach or other sturdy salad leaf

For the dressing:

2 tbsp tomato puree

1 tsp garlic paste

4 tbsp light cooking oil

1 tbsp lemon juice

1 tsp dried thyme or mixed herbs

1 tsp ground cumin

Couscous is a quick and simple base for a meal at any time of day – and it's not expensive to buy at all. Use it as a vehicle for scraps of veg, fruit and a handful of whatever spices you have to hand. I make a variation on this fairly regularly for packed lunches, evening snacks or when cooking just for myself, and it's comforting, filling and very good for you.

First make your dressing, so that's done and can be languishing around intensifying while you throw the couscous together. Measure the tomato puree into a small jar with a tight-fitting lid – the size of an average jam jar is perfect for this. Add the garlic and then the oil, lemon, herbs and cumin. Screw the lid on tight and shake vigorously until well combined, then set to one side.

Measure your onion and peppers into a large nonstick pan and grate in the carrot. Add the cooking oil and cook on a medium heat for a few minutes until the veg has softened. Drain and rinse your chickpeas and add them to the pan, along with the sultanas or raisins and couscous. Pour over the chicken stock and bring to the boil. When the liquid is bubbling, turn the heat off, stir everything together, then place a lid on top tightly. Leave to stand for 10 minutes for the couscous to absorb all the stock and become fluffy. Stir through the spinach, then pour over the dressing and enjoy hot or cold.

Store in the fridge in an airtight container or bag and consume within 3 days. Not suitable for freezing in its current state, but you can thin it out with more stock and any remaining dressing and make it into a soup that riffs on a minestrone, which is perfectly suitable for freezing.

Vegetable Chowder V

SERVES 4

1 tbsp light cooking oil

320g frozen onion or fresh if you're up to it

4 fat cloves of garlic, or 2 tbsp garlic paste

600ml chicken or vegetable stock

1 x 520g tin of potatoes, or 400g fresh potatoes

1 tsp plain flour

200ml milk

320g mixed frozen veg

lots of black pepper, to taste

This simple soup is made with just a handful of ingredients and is creamy, hearty and filling, while also very good for you. It contains three of your 5 a day – not bad for the work of a moment. Mrs J likes to slather hers in hot sauce, whereas I prefer a dash of lemon juice and a lot of black pepper on mine.

Warm the oil in a large nonstick pan and add the onion. If using fresh onion, dice it first before warming the pan, else the oil will get too hot and may start smoking. Cook on a very low heat for 10 minutes to soften without burning or browning. Finely chop the garlic and add to the pan, or the paste, then pour over the stock.

Dice the potatoes and add to the pan, then bring to the boil. Reduce to a simmer and cook for 10 minutes – 20 if using fresh potatoes – until they start to fall apart.

Remove half of the potatoes and onion from the pan into the large cup of a bullet blender or the jug of a standard blender. Cover with stock from the pan, then spoon in the flour. This is a completely lazy way of doing this, but it works just fine. Blend to a thick liquid, then pour back into the pan.

Add the milk and mixed frozen veg and warm through until the veg is soft. Season generously with pepper and serve piping hot.

Will keep for 3 days in the fridge in a clean airtight container, or 3 months in the freezer.

Crabby Nora

SERVES 1

80g spaghetti or
other pasta

1 fat clove of garlic,
or 1 tsp garlic paste

1 tbsp butter or light
cooking oil

1 large egg

60ml whole milk

30g hard strong
cheese

1 x 170g tin of crab
meat

salt and pepper, to
taste

This quick and irreverent take on a carbonara uses crab in place of the standard bacon – not for reasons of grandeur, but for a quick and simple meal. If you're feeling flush, use canned shredded crab meat, but if not, torn-up seafood sticks, tiny frozen prawns or a generous dollop of crab sandwich paste will do just fine.

Bring a pan of salted water to the boil. Add the pasta, reduce to a simmer, cover and cook for 8–10 minutes.

Chop the garlic clove into fine pieces and add this (or the garlic paste, if using) to a nonstick frying pan with the butter or oil and a pinch of salt. Cook on a gentle heat so as not to burn the garlic.

In a separate bowl, whisk the egg and milk, and grate in the cheese. Season generously with black pepper.

When the pasta is cooked, drain it and return to the pan. Add the cooked garlic, then drain the crab meat and stir it through the pasta quickly. Add the egg and cheese mixture and stir briskly and thoroughly; the heat from the pasta will lightly cook the egg and melt the cheese.

Serve immediately. It will keep in the fridge for 24 hours, but it is not recommended for freezing.

Blue Cheese and Pickled Herring Panzanella

SERVES 2, OR 1
FOR NOW AND 1
FOR LATER

2 slices of brown, wholemeal or granary bread

2 spring onions

1 jar of pickled rollmop herrings

100g crumbly blue cheese, like Stilton

handful of fresh parsley leaves

1 tbsp light cooking oil

lemon juice, to taste

salt and pepper, to taste

Inspired by one of the best starters at my most favourite restaurant, The Pipe of Port in Southend-on-Sea. A sprawling, sawdust-sprinkled cellar of conviviality, warm welcomes and hot pies, I have been enjoying this establishment for around fifteen years, and hope to continue to do so for many years to come. I was working on my local newspaper, the Southend Echo, in my early twenties when the call came in from the proprietor saying that they were going to put the restaurant up for sale. We dutifully ran the story and the outpouring of love and support from the local community was so great that within the week it was off the market because they had changed their minds. I make an effort to go as often as possible, which is far less than I'd like, and I have the toasts with pickled herring and blue cheese every single time. This panzanella is a tribute to many happy evenings there, without directly attempting to recreate something I love so much that I dare not fiddle with it.

First tear your bread into bite-sized pieces. You can slice it up if you prefer, but I like the rough edges and the physicality of breaking bread, possibly a hangover from my reckless youth in the congregation of the local Baptist church, or just a need to keep my hands busy. Pop your bread into a large mixing bowl.

Finely slice your spring onions, as small as you can get them, and add to the bowl.

Remove the rollmop herrings from the jar and remove any wooden sticks or stakes that may be holding them together. Not all brands use these, but it's worth spending a moment picking them out instead of accidentally eating one...

Slice the rollmops into small chunks and add to the bowl. Crumble in your cheese. Roughly chop your parsley leaves and scatter through. Season with salt and plenty of pepper, a drizzle of oil and a dash or two of lemon juice. Toss everything together and leave to stand for 10 minutes to marinate and for the bread to soak up all of the various flavours.

Enjoy on the day of preparation. If making in advance, store the bread separately and combine just before serving.

Hot Nicoise

1 x 145g tin of tuna
in oil

1 x 520g tin of cooked
baby potatoes

1 onion, thinly sliced

2 tbsp black olives

4 medium eggs

a few handfuls of
baby spinach or
other fresh salad
leaves

For the dressing:

2 tbsp oil (from tuna
tin)

½ tsp mustard

1 tbsp honey

1 tbsp any light
vinegar

a pinch of dried
mixed herbs

salt and pepper, to
taste

I like the concept of a Nicoise salad, but the reality generally leaves me feeling short-changed and slightly hungry. This is a more substantial and probably entirely blasphemous version, served hot and hefty.

First drain the tuna carefully over a small bowl or mug, reserving the oil. You'll use this for cooking and for the dressing. If your tuna didn't come in oil, don't worry, just use a light cooking oil instead.

Drain and halve your potatoes and pop them in a large nonstick pan with a tablespoon of oil. Add the onion, and cook over medium heat for a few minutes, nudging with a wooden spoon or spatula to disturb. The potatoes can spit a little because they hold a lot of water from the tin, so watch out!

While the potatoes and onion are cooking, make your dressing. Measure 2 tablespoons of oil into a small jar with a lid. Add the mustard, honey and vinegar and a pinch of herbs. Season lightly with salt and pepper, then screw the lid on tight and shake it well to combine. Remove the lid and set it to one side.

When the potatoes are starting to turn a golden colour, tip in the tuna and olives, and stir well to distribute. Crack the eggs into the pan and cover quickly. Turn the heat down to low for 6–8 minutes until the eggs cook to your liking. Add the spinach or salad leaves 20 seconds before serving to wilt. Serve with the dressing and extra black pepper.

Eat immediately, the fried eggs won't keep very well. If you're planning to make this in advance, or live alone, use boiled eggs in place of fried and it will keep for a day in the fridge. Reheat gently, or eat cold.

Use the best tinned potatoes you can stretch to for this one; it's one of the few occasions where it's worth splashing out ever so slightly.

My favourite way to cook is the one-pan meal; I started cooking like this when I was a single mum on benefits, because it's more energy efficient to pop everything in on one hob, but also because one-pan meals tend to create what I lovingly term 'bowl food' – meals that can be consumed with a bowl tucked into the crook of my arm while I watch something mindless and trashy on the television. Sometimes I just carry the whole pan to the couch and sit it on a cushion so as not to burn my lap, then get stuck in. Less washing up, that way.

ONE PAN

Mashed Potatoes V

In the inimitable but oft-imitated (as you see here) style of the greatly missed and dearly beloved Anthony Bourdain

SHOULD SERVE 4.
FREQUENTLY DOES
NOT

500g potatoes

150g butter

40ml double cream

salt and pepper,
to taste

If you've ever wondered why restaurant mashed potatoes are so irresistibly delicious, it's because they are generally one-part butter to three-part potato. I remember making them for the first time in a restaurant kitchen in Exmouth Market, transfixed by just how much butter a pile of potatoes could take. These potatoes, a tweak on an Anthony Bourdain recipe, are my favourites, and the only ones that will do for me in a time of emotional crisis. I'd like to pretend I halve the recipe or share it, but reader, I would be being dishonest with you.

I rarely advocate peeling potatoes for mash, typically preferring them rough and ready, but just this once, I defer to the French way of doing things.

So, peel your potatoes, and dice them into around 2cm chunks for a faster cooking time. Place in a large saucepan and cover with cold water, generously salted. Bring to the boil, then reduce to a simmer until cooked – around 15 minutes, depending on the variety of potatoes used.

Drain the potatoes, and return to the pan. Mash vigorously, then add a quarter of the butter and mash again. Repeat until your mash is very smooth and all the butter has been incorporated, then stir in the cream. Season to taste and serve immediately.

GOOD FOOD FOR BAD DAYS

Lighter Mashed Potatoes V

SERVES 4

500g potatoes

100g light mayonnaise

salt and pepper, to taste

If the previous recipe for potatoes, with two-thirds of a packet of butter in, made you feel slightly nauseated, then this one may be more up your street . Only slightly less rich than the original, the mayo makes it creamier and lighter in flavour.

First peel your potatoes, if you'd rather, or don't if you prefer a rougher texture and a little more fibre to your spuds. (If you aren't peeling them, give them a good scrub under the tap.)

Dice your spuds and pop them into a large saucepan. Cover with water and season generously with salt. Bring to the boil on your largest hob ring, then reduce to a simmer. Simmer for 15 minutes, or until cooked soft.

Drain your potatoes thoroughly, then return them to the pan. Mash vigorously until they form a rough paste, then add a third of the mayonnaise. Mash again until the mayo is incorporated, then repeat twice more.

Season to taste and serve hot.

Meatball and White Bean Stew

SERVES 4
GENEROUSLY

1 large onion

6 fat cloves of garlic, or 2 tbsp garlic paste

1 tbsp oil

1 x 400g tin of chopped tomatoes

400ml chicken, veg or ham stock, or use a stock cube and water

500g tinned potatoes

200g tinned sliced carrots

1 x 400g tin of meatballs in tomato sauce

1 x 400g tin of white beans

1 tsp dried mixed herbs

1 tbsp light-coloured vinegar

salt and pepper, to serve

This is a hearty, simple supper, so much more than the sum of its parts. Meatballs in a tin may be considered childish, but they make for a quick and easy standby, and because they are already cooked through in the canning process, this dish can be thrown together in mere minutes. As with all tomato-based stews, it benefits from a resting period to develop the flavour, so if you have time, allow it to cool completely, then bring back to the heat to serve. I used black-eyed beans in mine when I first made this, as it's what I had to hand at the time, but butter beans would be more substantial and cannellini will break down to give a creamy base note. So really, any bean will do.

First, peel and roughly dice your onion and toss into a large pan. Peel and slice your garlic, or measure in the paste. Add the oil, stir, bring to a gentle heat and cook for a few minutes to start to soften.

Pour in the tomatoes and add the stock – or water and a stock cube. Drain and halve the potatoes and add to the pan with the drained carrots, then add the meatballs, including the tomato sauce from the tin. Drain the white beans and add those too. Stir in the herbs and vinegar and season with salt and pepper. Bring to the boil very briefly, then reduce to a simmer and cook for 10–15 minutes to warm through. And that's it! You can cook it for longer if you want to, to thicken the sauce and develop the flavour, but it's ready to eat from now if you like.

Keeps for 2 days in the fridge in an airtight container. Not recommended for freezing.

Butter Bean, Brown Lentil and Red Wine Casserole V

SERVES 4

200g onion (about 2 medium onions), chopped

1 whole head of garlic, or 3 tbsp garlic paste

500g diced carrot and swede

1 x 400g tin of butter beans

1 x 400g tin of brown lentils

400g passata or chopped tomatoes

100ml red wine

800ml chicken-style or vegetable stock

1 tbsp balsamic vinegar

1 tbsp dried mixed herbs

A hearty slow-cooked dinner that freezes well, so if you aren't feeding four, parcel some up into freezable bags or containers for some healthy homemade ready meals, handy for days when you aren't up to cooking from scratch. The flavour improves with a rest, and I wholeheartedly empathize.

Pop the onion into a large nonstick pan, preferably one with a lid. Peel the garlic and halve the cloves lengthways or dollop in the paste. Add the carrot and swede. Drain and thoroughly rinse the butter beans and brown lentils and add those too. The pan should be entirely off the heat at this stage.

Pour over the passata or chopped tomatoes, then add the wine, stock, balsamic vinegar and herbs. Bring to the boil on your largest hob ring, then reduce to a simmer, move to the smallest hob ring and cover. Cook for 45 minutes over the lowest heat on the smallest hob, stirring occasionally to disturb the ingredients at the bottom of the pan. Top up with a splash of water as required.

You can continue to cook it for a further 30 minutes if you like and have the patience and means to do so, but it is perfectly delicious from this point onwards.

Will keep in the fridge for up to 3 days, or the freezer for 3 months. Can be microwaved from frozen; cook on full power for 5 minutes, stir, then cook on full power for 4 minutes. Ensure it is thoroughly piping hot throughout before serving – microwave times may vary depending on power and model.

Peri Peri Black Bean Soup

MAKES 4 GENEROUS PORTIONS

120g onion (about 1 large onion)

1 whole small head of garlic

1 tbsp oil

1 x 400g tin of black beans

1 x 400g tin of black-eyed beans or pinto beans

1 x 400g tin of chopped tomatoes

600ml chicken stock

6 tbsp medium peri peri sauce

It's 2014. I'm living in London, working as part of a consultancy job for a high-street chain of popular restaurants. The night is frenzied; sixteen or seventeen dishes strewn across the table, on high chairs, the coffee table, cooling on the front doorstep. I scrawl notes on yellow index cards in slopey italics, spattering them with oil and paprika and three kinds of chilli, burning one at the edges in my reckless enthusiasm. It's my first big job of this nature, and I'm a nameless entity, a silent partner, but my ideas are manifested before my eyes, and if I do well, they'll end up on dinner plates across the nation. Unusually for me, I'm not nervous. I'm in my element, creating food to share, and for appraisal. I'm desperately lonely in London, forty miles from my friends and family, invisible on the pavements, unknown at the local pubs. I just want someone to tell me I did well, and so, I work through the night, testing and tasting and tweaking and writing, until I can do no more.

The original had shredded chicken folded through at the end; you can do this if you like, but I don't feel it's necessary. You can eat this as a hearty soup, reduce it down for a casserole, have it cold in tortilla wraps, on toast, in toasted sandwiches with lashings of cheese, on top of a jacket potato, or any other way you see fit.

First peel and finely slice your onions and pop into a large saucepan, preferably one with a heavy bottom. Peel the garlic and halve the cloves lengthways, then add them to the pan. Pour over the oil and place on a low heat. Cook gently for 10 minutes, stirring occasionally, until the onion and garlic start to soften.

Drain and thoroughly rinse both cans of beans, and tip into the pan. Pour over the chopped tomatoes, then the stock. Bring to the boil, then reduce to a simmer, stirring well. Add the peri peri sauce, stir again, and cook for 40 minutes, until the beans are very soft and falling apart and the liquid has reduced by a third. Eat immediately, or allow to cool completely and chill until needed.

This keeps in the fridge for up to 3 days and just improves the longer it's left there – although not for longer than 3 days, as it starts to deteriorate after that. To keep it longer, cool completely, then pop it in the freezer. To microwave from frozen in an 800W oven, microwave on High for 4 minutes, stir and leave to stand for a minute, then microwave on High for 4 minutes more. You may need to adjust the timings to suit your microwave, so these are approximate.

Mushrooms and Anchovies

MAKES 2
GENEROUS
PORTIONS

1 large onion, red
or white

90g tin or jar of
anchovies in oil

400g fresh
mushrooms (the
meatier the better)

1 tsp thyme,
rosemary or dried
mixed herbs

1 tbsp butter (or an
extra tbsp oil)

1 tsp vinegar (white,
red wine or cider are
best, but any will do
at a pinch)

black pepper, to taste

I toyed with calling this dish 'mushrooms in anchovy sauce' or 'anchovies in mushroom sauce' but neither quite fitted nor did it justice. It needs a base of butter-soft blandness to temper its wildness of flavour, so serve it atop a pile of creamy mash or plain pasta, and enjoy. The bolder the mushrooms the better the finished product, so choose from farmhouse, baby portobello, shiitake, wild, ceps or a mixture of whatever you can find. Plain white standard mushrooms also work, if you can't find a bolder variety, but the more exotic ones are worth seeking out.

First peel your onion and finely slice it. (I use a mandolin to make short work of this, and a pair of ski goggles to protect my eyes, because sometimes chopping onions can be overwhelmingly off-putting. Of course, you can also use bags of frozen sliced onions, and I do that too, but for the sake of writing a recipe book and Seeming Proper, I'm pretending here that we start with a whole onion.)

Toss your onion into a wide, shallow nonstick pan. Open the tin or jar of anchovies carefully and pour their oil into the pan over the onions, then set the anchovies to one side for a moment. Set the pan over medium heat and gently cook the onions for 7–8 minutes, stirring intermittently to disturb them so they cook evenly and do not stick or burn.

Meanwhile, slice your mushrooms to around 3mm thick. Add these to the pan and stir in. Tip in your anchovies and break them up roughly with the side of your wooden spoon, and stir through along with the herbs. Add the butter or oil and cook for a further 10 minutes, turning the heat down to low when the mushrooms start to soften.

Finish with the vinegar, and stir through. Season to taste with black pepper – it will be plenty salty enough with the residual anchovy – and serve over your carb of choice.

This is one of those dishes that is even better the next day, so if you have any left, allow it to cool then chill in the fridge, then warm back through thoroughly to serve. It doesn't freeze particularly well as it isn't very saucy, but it will keep for 48 hours in the fridge. Any longer and the mushrooms start to turn a little sluggish, which isn't pleasant.

The deep, rich flavours of both anchovy and mushroom don't jostle for attention here, rather they languish, complementing one another in a mouth party so sumptuous it oughtn't to be allowed at all.

Recalibration Supper VE

MAKES 4 PORTIONS

2 large onions, or 240g frozen sliced onions

6 fat cloves of garlic, or 2 tbsp garlic paste

1 large leek, or 140g frozen sliced leeks

1 large carrot, or 1 x 300g tin sliced or baby carrots

oil, for frying

1 x 400g tin of borlotti beans

400ml chicken or vegetable stock

1 x 400g tin of chopped tomatoes

1 tbsp wine or cider vinegar

200g kale, spinach or other dark leafy greens, finely chopped

salt and pepper, to taste

The veg in this bowl can be changed to suit whatever you have in the fridge or cupboard at the time, so long as the quantities of each remain roughly the same. You can swap the carrots for potato, parsnip, squash or any other sturdy root vegetable; the greens for finely shredded cabbage or leafy greens, any beans, any grains; and the onions and leeks are interchangeable. It's more of a formula for a bowl of balanced goodness than a prescriptive recipe. I make a version of this depending on whatever I have to hand, always slightly different but comfortingly familiar, and packed with vitamins and gentle nutrition. It's my pick-me-up after any period of illness or exhaustion, and it's popular with the whole family. I call it our 'recalibration supper', but it's good for any time of day. It can be eaten cold over pasta with cheese on top, but it's best served hot and by the largest bowl you can find.

First peel and finely slice your onions or measure out the frozen onions. Add the onion – in whatever guise – to a large nonstick pan. Peel your garlic and halve it lengthways, then add to the pan, or add the paste. Thinly slice your leek and carrot and add those too, or chuck in the ready sliced veg. Drizzle over a little oil, and season with salt and pepper. Cook over medium heat for 5–6 minutes to start to soften.

Drain and thoroughly rinse the beans and tip into the pan. Pour over the stock and bring to the boil. Reduce to a simmer, then stir in the tomatoes and vinegar. Cover and simmer over low heat for

GOOD FOOD FOR BAD DAYS

15 minutes, until thick and glossy. Toss in the greens and wilt for 30 seconds (spinach) to a few minutes (kale and spring greens).

Serve warm with bread and butter, torn up and dunked.

Keeps well in the fridge for up to 3 days. Can be frozen for up to 3 months. Defrost completely and reheat through before serving.

Five-a-Day Soup, Three Ways

MAKES 2 VERY
GENEROUS
PORTIONS

1 large onion

2 decent-sized carrots

4 fat cloves of garlic, or 6 smaller ones

1 large courgette, or 2 smaller ones

1 x 400g tin of cannellini beans, or haricot or pinto beans

1 x 400g tin or carton of chopped tomatoes

500ml chicken or vegetable stock

1 tbsp dried mixed herbs

black pepper, to taste

Whenever I make soup in my household I end up making it three different ways. Mrs J likes hers left completely unblended and chunky, a broth with beans and vegetables in. Small Boy has his pureed to smooth, and usually as a pasta sauce baked beneath a pile of cheese. I like mine somewhere between the two; a thick blended base with a smattering of veg and beans in it for interest and texture. This recipe provides a full slate of five of your 5 a day if you eat half of the quantity given here, which is admittedly a generous bowlful, but it does a lot of good for very little effort. If energy levels are low or time is on the short side, swap the carrots for a can of sliced or baby carrots, the onion for frozen diced onion and the garlic for garlic paste, to make it faster and simpler, but just as nutritious.

First, peel and slice the onion and toss into a large saucepan. Roughly chop your carrots and add those too. Peel your garlic cloves and quarter them lengthways. Dice the courgette and add to the pan. Drain and thoroughly rinse the beans and tip over the top, then pour over the tomatoes and stock.

Bring to the boil, then reduce to a simmer. Measure in the herbs and cover the pan with a lid, or some foil or a larger pan if you don't have a lid. Simmer for 30 minutes, until the veg is very soft. Season to taste with black pepper.

If you like, you can serve it chunky, like a casserole or stew, or you can remove half and pulse it to smooth in a bullet blender, then return it to the pan and combine it with the remaining veg and broth. Or, for a completely smooth soup that can be repurposed as a pasta sauce, blend the whole lot, probably in batches, and warm back through to serve.

Keeps in a sealed container in the fridge for 3 days or the freezer for 3 months.

Puttanesca Funebra

SERVES 1, TWICE

100g onion (about 1 medium onion)

2 fat cloves of garlic

4–6 anchovies from a tin or jar, to taste, plus 1 tbsp of oil

1 x 400g tin of chopped tomatoes

a hefty pinch of chilli flakes

a dash of vinegar, any kind

200g black spaghetti

grated cheese, to serve (optional)

'Funebra' is Italian for 'Funeral' – and as far as I am aware, Funereal Puttanesca isn't yet a dish that exists in mainstream cookery writing or parlance, but I made this with inky black pasta and immediately knew I wanted to make it again. For when you need dinner as black as your heart, as hot as your temper, as salty as your uncried tears, as sour as your mood, this is just the ticket. Throw it together in minutes and marvel briefly at its bewitching blackness, before scoffing the lot with noisy slurps. If you don't have charcoal pasta to hand – and I admit it is a fairly niche ingredient – you can make a standard puttanesca and just eat it in the dark or something.

First, peel and finely dice your onions, and toss into a large nonstick pan. Peel and finely chop your garlic and add that too. Pour in the anchovies and 1 tablespoon of their oil, add the chopped tomatoes, the chilli and the vinegar and cook for 15 minutes until the sauce is thick and glossy. Remove from the heat and set to one side to cool and settle.

Bring a pan of generously salted water to the boil, then reduce to a simmer. Snap your spaghetti in half – because it's easier to cook – and add to the pan. Simmer for 8–10 minutes, or according to the packet instructions, until tender. Drain and return to the pan, along with the puttanesca sauce, and warm through briefly to serve. Serve with grated cheese, if you like.

Keeps in a sealed container in the fridge for 2 days; loosen with a dash of oil or basic dressing to prevent the pasta from sticking together before refrigerating. Not recommended for freezing.

Beer Mac and Cheese

SERVES 2, GENEROUSLY

330ml beer

300ml chicken stock

160g onion, chopped (about 1 large onion)

½ tsp mustard, any

200g macaroni pasta

80g mature Cheddar

1 slice of bread

This recipe was inspired by one that Emma Freud cooked in BBC Good Food magazine a year or so ago, which has haunted me ever since. I'd be sitting at my desk and it would pop into my head. I'd be minding my own business and there it would be, front and foremost in my subconscious. I'd be drifting off to sleep and it would whisper to me in the dark. Until I could take it no longer, and I had to make my own version. This is a simple sling-it-in one pan edition; I toyed with adding full-fat milk to temper the tang of the beer, but decided I quite liked it. You may wish to, however, depending on how accustomed you are to the taste of warm beer.

Pour the beer and stock into a medium saucepan. Add the onion and mustard. Bring to the boil, then reduce to a simmer.

Measure in your pasta and cover the pan with a lid, or tin foil or a plate will do. Simmer for 10 minutes, disturbing once to stir to prevent the pasta from sticking.

When the pasta is cooked and almost all of the beer and stock is absorbed, grate in most of the Cheddar and stir well to melt it.

Grate or blitz the bread to crumbs and scatter on top. Add the remaining cheese, and serve. If I'm feeling fancy, I like to sometimes decant the cheesy, beery pasta to an ovenproof dish and finish it under the grill for a cheesy crusty top, but it's not essential and just creates more washing up, which I can't always justify…. But sometimes, just sometimes, it's worth it.

Will keep for 2 days in the fridge. Not recommended for freezing – you can, but it's not quite the same afterwards.

Borlottouille (Bor-lo-too-ee)

SERVES 2

1 large onion

4 fat cloves of garlic

1 large courgette

1 tbsp cooking oil

1 x 400g tin of chopped tomatoes

250ml stock – veg, chicken or beef

1 tsp light-coloured vinegar

1 tsp dried mixed herbs

1 x 400g tin of borlotti beans

salt and pepper, to taste

This is partly a ratatouille, partly a borlotti bean stew, hence the portmanteau. I was inspired, once again, by a recipe from the wonderful Sarah Raven – her Garden Cookbook *is my go-to for all seasons and ingredients. She calls this her 'absolute favourite recipe for borlotti beans', so I absolutely had to try it. I have tinkered and tweaked it; she uses fresh beans and tomatoes, as is her way; I use tinned, as is mine. Sarah uses fresh coriander in hers but I cannot stand the taste of it, so I have used dried mixed herbs and added a splash of vinegar.*

Peel and finely slice the onion and garlic, and toss them into a large, heavy-bottomed nonstick pan. Dice your courgette small, and add that too. Measure in the oil, season with salt and pepper and cook slowly and gently for 10 minutes on the lowest burner until the veg starts to soften.

Pour over the chopped tomatoes and the stock, then add the vinegar and herbs. Give it all a stir to gently combine, keeping it on a low heat.

Drain and thoroughly rinse the borlotti beans and stir them in. Simmer everything together for 40 minutes, topping up with a splash of water if needed so that the beans don't dry out until the sauce is thick and glossy and the beans are ever-so soft.

Serve warm on rice, toast, pasta, or just spooned from the pan into your mouth, which is absolutely my preferred method.

Will keep in the fridge in an airtight container for 3 days, or in the freezer for 3 months.

GOOD FOOD FOR BAD DAYS

Sausage, Swede and Cider Sling-It-In

**SERVES 4,
EASILY FROZEN**

6 sausages

oil, for cooking

120g onion or frozen
sliced onions

1 large leek, or 150g
frozen sliced leek

2 celery stalks
(optional)

150g swede, or
1 large potato

2 medium carrots

200ml cider

400ml water

1 chicken, ham or veg
stock cube, or 2 tsp
bouillon powder

1 tsp English
mustard

4 tbsp dried sage and
onion stuffing mix

1 x 400g tin of baked
beans

2 tsp any light
vinegar or lemon
juice, to serve

salt and pepper,
to taste

*This is a comforting one-pot dinner that evokes all of
the flavours of pub classics and Sunday roasts, but with
a fraction of the work. The stuffing crumbs are one of my
favourite ingredients – the* Guardian *once did a feature
on my love affair with it, which involved a photoshoot
where I bent perilously close over a smoking briefcase and
had a waterfall of crumbs poured on my head. Thankfully,
in my kitchen these crumbs just live in a large jar and
nobody throws them at my face, but I do hurl them into
a surprising number of suppers. Here they do a lot of
heavy lifting; thickening the sauce and adding a deep,
herby base note.*

*You can play with the cider and water quantities,
depending on who you're cooking for, as long as the total
liquid content is 600ml. For the purposes of this recipe,
the frozen carrot and swede mix works well if wrestling
with a solid and rather graceless root vegetable just isn't
what you feel like doing. And I don't blame you, swedes
are absolute gits. I use a cheap plastic and metal
guillotine-style contraption to pulverize them into
neat little cubes these days (see the Fairly Essential
Equipment list on page 24 for more details) and it's
extremely satisfying!*

First, pop your sausages into a large nonstick pan and drizzle with the oil. Cook over a medium heat for 5–6 minutes, hustling them around the pan every now and then to prevent them from sticking and burning.

Peel and dice your onion and leek if using fresh ones, or measure them out if using frozen. Finely slice the celery, if you're using it – it's not essential, but it does help bulk the dish out and adds a bright base note, as well as being packed with vitamins K, A and C, so it's worth bunging it into a dinner whenever you get the chance. Dice your swede or potato and carrots.

Add all the veg to the pan and extra oil, if required. Season with a pinch of salt. Cook for 10 minutes more, still jostling it all about every now and then.

Pour over the cider, wait a beat for it to settle, then add most of the water and the stock cube, mustard and stuffing mix. Drain and thoroughly rinse the beans, then add those too. Bring to the boil, then reduce to a simmer and cover. Cook for 25 minutes until the sausages and veg are cooked through and the sauce is thick and succulent. Add the remaining water, if required.

Finish with a dash of vinegar or lemon juice, and serve. I like to remove the sausages and chop them into slices, as it makes for a more pleasurable eating experience than wresting an entire banger into your chops, and it also makes it feel like the meat goes further. If I'm feeling fancy, I'll sling a handful of chopped greens, frozen spinach or kale in there too, for a bit of extra goodness.

I have written in previous books about the therapeutic nature of baking bread or stirring risotto. My close friends and family know me and my moods well enough by now to be firm with me, prodding me towards the kitchen when I start to withdraw into myself or am inexplicably sad.

The times I least feel like cooking are usually the times when disappearing into a cloud of steam and spices is exactly what I need, so I hope you find these recipes somewhat helpful, too.

Cooking just for yourself is the ultimate act of self-care; you are acknowledging that you are important enough to take time over, to nourish, to give pleasure to. It doesn't have to be complicated or a *Masterchef* masterpiece, it just needs to fill the hole. You wouldn't let anyone you love skip meals and refuse to feed themselves, so maybe you should gently remind yourself that you are worth taking the time over, too.

TAKE YOUR TIME

Better Soda Bread v

400ml full-fat milk or creamy plant-based milk of choice

1 tbsp lemon juice or any light vinegar

200g wholemeal flour

200g self-raising white flour, plus extra for dusting

1 tsp bicarbonate of soda

a pinch of salt

oil, for greasing

I have written many times about the therapeutic nature of baking bread with my bare hands – the pounding, pummelling and stretching that kneading requires is an excellent workout for nervous energy, both mental and physical, as is the slow rise and the soft yeasty scent that permeates my home as the dough starts to rise. But sometimes there isn't time, or energy, or there's a soup on the back burner and I want something a little more instantaneous. Soda bread is a brilliant standby for these occasions, with no kneading nor rising time, it's as close to instant gratification as breadmaking gets. This half-and-half version is a compromise between the goodness of wholemeal and the deliciousness of white bread; you can adjust the flours to suit your personal tastes or storecupboard, as long as they add up to 400g. Wholemeal is a little thirstier than white flour, as the husks absorb a considerable amount of liquid, so adjust your liquid quantities as required.

First, preheat your oven to 180°C/160°C fan/gas 4 and ensure there is a shelf in the middle.

Measure your milk into a jug and add the lemon juice or vinegar. Stand it to one side for a moment to start to curdle.

Weigh the flours into a large mixing bowl and add the bicarbonate of soda and a pinch of salt. Stir through briskly to evenly distribute the bicarb; this helps for an even rise and stops it congregating in a little bitter pile somewhere – which is deeply unpleasant to bite into!

Make a well in the centre – like a shallow wide hole – and pour the curdling milk into it. Mix well to form a thick sticky batter, not a pliable dough – not for this recipe.

Lightly grease and flour a 450g loaf tin and scrape the batter into it. Jostle it gently from side to side to sort of level the top, then place it into the oven. Bake for 40 minutes, or until risen and a sharp knife inserted into the centre comes away clean. If it doesn't, return it to the oven for 10 minutes more, covering the top with tin foil to prevent it from browning.

Remove from the oven and cool in the tin for 30 minutes before removing – the residual heat will continue to cook the centre a little more, and if you remove it too early, it could crumble, which would be a delicious shame.

Courgette Farrotto V

MAKES 4
GENEROUS
PORTIONS

1 large onion

4 fat cloves of garlic
or 6 smaller ones

2 celery stalks
(non-essential, but a
decent addition)

1 tbsp oil or butter

1 rudely large
courgette or
2 smaller ones

300g quick-cook
farro

200ml white wine or
cider

400ml chicken or veg
stock

4 tbsp cream cheese,
any kind

hard strong cheese,
to taste

black pepper, to taste

Farrotto is like risotto, only it takes a quarter of the time to cook. Which is ideal when you want all the creamy comforting of the classic Italian dinner yet have none of the time or inclination to babysit it. Farro is an ancient grain that is so mystical and desirable it's sold in such far-flung climes as my local Tesco and Asda. Feted by cookie-cutter-thin and beautiful wellness bloggers the world over, I picked it up not for its enthusiastic magical properties, but because it said 'quick cook' on the packet, and those are two little words to seduce me by. In a culinary manner, of course. This recipe is delicious hot, straight from the pan, but also cold the next morning, when the farro has softened even more and the flavours have developed. So make a batch of it and eat it for days – you won't regret it.

First peel and finely slice your onion and toss it into a wide, nonstick shallow pan. Peel the garlic, quarter it lengthways and add that too. Finely slice the celery and add to the mix, then drizzle over the oil or dollop in the butter. Bring the pan to medium-low heat and stir intermittently for a couple of minutes to start to soften the onion and veg.

Finely slice your courgette – I use a mandolin for mine, as it's quick and efficient, as well as cheaper to buy and more reliable than a decent knife. Add to the pan and stir briefly.

Tip in the farro and stir. Leave for a minute, then pour over the wine or cider. Wait a minute for it to absorb, then add two-thirds of the stock and the cream cheese, and stir well. Cover and bring to the boil, then reduce to a simmer.

Cook the farro for 10–12 minutes until soft and swollen, adding the remaining stock as required. Grate over the hard cheese and finish with plenty of black pepper to serve.

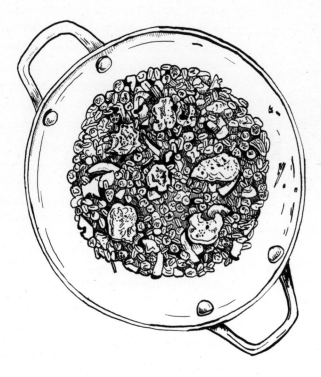

Pub Chicken Vindaloo

MAKES 4 PORTIONS

1 large onion

6 fat cloves of garlic

4 tbsp butter, ghee or light cooking oil

3cm piece of fresh root ginger, peeled

1 tsp ground cinnamon

½ tsp chilli flakes

1 tbsp garam masala

2 tsp ground cumin

300g skinless and boneless chicken breast

400g passata or chopped tomatoes

1 tsp mustard – English or whatever you have to hand

1 tbsp sugar

1 tbsp lemon juice

1 tbsp white wine vinegar

September 2019. I've taken myself to a local pub to work – this may seem overly testing behaviour for a recovering alcoholic, but I like to sit in the corner and drink lime cordial and write. At home, I find things to do, I am restless, I am obsessively folding tea towels and making messes just to clear them up again. Working from home is a relentless irony; never quite fully working, never really feeling at home, and so I have a roster of local establishments that I frequent, plugging in my laptop and sitting still and quietly in a way that I cannot when I am alone. Curious eyes flicker towards me from time to time, but I don't meet them. I have things to do.

Peckish, I rove through the menu. It's Thursday, so it's Curry Night. I contemplate ordering the chicken vindaloo. I don't know why. Even now, I don't know why. I'm setting myself a test that I can't possibly excel in. It arrives, with a fresh pint of lime cordial, plenty of ice. I dip a tentative fork in the sauce, gauging it for its viciousness. It's ... fine. I have some more. And then some more. And then suddenly my eyes are streaming, and the tears I have longed for for days are falling down my reddening face. This is the catharsis that I needed. My mouth is on fire. I demolish my garlic naan almost whole, an ineffectual fire blanket for my burning lips and tongue. My nose is running, I wipe it on my napkin. I finger the ice from my cordial and suck on it slowly, silently mourning its disappearance as it all too swiftly vanishes, the temporary trail of relief quickly gone. I mix the remaining vindaloo with the rice to temper it, and slowly, painfully, finish the lot. Three forkfuls of vindaloo and rice, one ice cube. A nose blow. A silent sob into my notebook. And repeat, and repeat, and repeat, until spent.

You may wish to replace the chicken with a vegetable to make a vegetarian version. I can recommend thinly sliced aubergine or mushroom for a hearty texture.

Some notes: room-temperature vindaloo is a lot less of an assault on your senses than a piping-hot one. And drinking a fizzy drink alongside a hell-hot curry is a very bad idea. If you don't fancy sobbing openly over your dinner or feeling like you may actually combust, you can tone down the chilli and enjoy the flavour base notes without the impending sense of flammable doom. And make enough to freeze, in portions, for those moments where you feel yourself needing a good cry but can't quite make it happen. It's cheaper than therapy, at any rate. Finally, eating a sliced fridge-cold apple immediately after this curry is a sensation so beatific I can barely find the words for it. Like a thousand kisses from sweet, honeyed angels for your burned and shrieking skin. Better yet, apple and vanilla ice cream.

RECIPE OVER THE PAGE →

First peel your onion and slice it as finely as you can. Toss it into a large nonstick pan. Peel and mince or very finely slice your garlic and add that too. Add the fat (butter, ghee or cooking oil) and grate in the ginger, then cook together on a low heat for a minute. Add all of the spices and stir well to evenly distribute.

Dice your chicken breast into roughly 3cm chunks and add to the pan. Turn the heat up to medium and cook for 6–8 minutes, turning intermittently to seal on all sides.

When the chicken is sealed, pour over the passata or tomatoes, then add the mustard, sugar, lemon juice and vinegar. Continue to cook, stirring well so it doesn't catch and burn, for another 6–8 minutes, before turning the heat down to low and cooking for 20 minutes more. This allows the flavours to develop and the onion and garlic to soften and sweeten. If you want to cook it for even longer, it will only improve – but I'm acutely aware that not all of us have the time, nor disposable funds, to fritter away on hours over the stove, so 20 minutes will suffice if that's all you have.

This is one of those dishes that gets better for a cooling-off period, so cook it in advance if you are able, and allow it to cool completely, before gently reheating to serve.

Will keep in the fridge in an airtight container for 3 days, or in the freezer for 3 months. Defrost completely overnight in the fridge and reheat to piping hot before serving.

Beer Pizza V

MAKES 2 THIN
25CM PIZZAS

For the dough:

100g wholemeal flour

150g white flour, plus
extra for dusting

10g dried active yeast

a pinch of salt

1 tsp sugar

125ml beer

oil, for greasing

For the sauce:

1 x 400g tin of
chopped tomatoes

1 tbsp vinegar

a pinch of salt

1 tbsp garlic paste

1 tbsp dried mixed
herbs, plus extra to
serve

plus 1 ball of
mozzarella and 80g
mature Cheddar,
chilli flakes and
black pepper, to top

I have made many, many pizzas in my short life so far, and eaten many more of them, and I have to say, as immodest and irritating as it may sound, that this is one of my favourite recipes. So much so, I remade it three days running, ostensibly to make sure that I had the recipe right, but really because I couldn't stop thinking about it. There's something therapeutic about making pizza dough; grinding your palms into it, shoving it across the worktop, stretching it and kneading it and then leaving it well alone to recover.... And at the end of it all, you have a pizza to enjoy!

As a nod to health I have used half wholemeal flour in this recipe; if adapting it back to all white flour, reduce the liquid a little, as wholemeal is huskier and thirstier than its bleached brethren. Blitzing the flour in a blender may seem a little ostentatious, but the finer grind makes for a more supple and superior dough, so skip this step at your peril. I discovered it on a whim, and now annoyingly I feel the need to do it every time I make it.

First pop the flours into the large cup of a bullet blender and blend for 30 seconds. Pause, give it a shake and blend again. This grinds the flour down finely, a sort of a cheat between the cheapest stuff and the finest 00 flour that other chefs recommend – it works to make your pizza dough more pliable, and crisper, and just, better. You can skip this step if it seems like an unnecessary fanny, but it helps merge the wholemeal and white flours together and lose the dry husky bits, if you need any further convincing.

Sift the flour into a large mixing bowl, then add the yeast, salt and sugar. Measure the beer into a microwave-safe jug and heat on High for 30 seconds, until it's warm to a tentative finger, but not too hot. Pour it into the mixing bowl and mix well with an oiled butter knife or silicone spatula to form your dough.

Heavily flour your worktop and tip the dough onto it. Knead for a few minutes until it starts to feel springy in your hands. Return it to the mixing bowl, cover it, and leave somewhere warm to rise for 2 hours, or until doubled in size. I am lucky to have an

GOOD FOOD FOR BAD DAYS

airing cupboard in my current rented house, with a hot water immersion tank in it, so I pop mine in there and it is done in what feels like no time at all.

While the dough rises, make your pizza sauce; the flavours will develop and benefit from a rest, so get this on as quickly as you can. Blend the tomatoes to smooth in a bullet blender or the jug of a standard blender, and pour into a medium heavy-bottomed saucepan. Add the vinegar, salt, garlic and herbs and cook gently over low heat for 20 minutes, or until thick and glossy. Remove from the heat and allow to cool completely.

When your dough is risen, turn your oven on to 220°C/200°C fan/gas 7, and place two shelves close together in the middle. Lightly grease two baking trays – I use a spray of Frylight or a dab of oil spread thinly with a pastry brush. Tip your dough out onto your worktop, reflouring it if you need to (mine is usually still floury from its previous outing!). Halve the dough, and gently knock each half into a ball. Roll out swiftly until as thin as you can bear it, then carefully transfer each base to each baking tray. (I use a sharp heavy knife to gently lift it from the worktop and the flat of my hand to quickly transport it to the tray. Don't worry if it stretches out of shape slightly in the process.)

Top each base with 2 tablespoons of sauce and divide the mozzarella between each pizza. Grate Cheddar over the top and finish with a pinch each of dried herbs, chilli and black pepper. Bake for 8–10 minutes, until sizzling, golden and crispy, and serve immediately.

Cooked pizzas will keep in the fridge for 24 hours, loosely covered. Warm through gently but thoroughly before serving.

Brown Rice Avgolemono with Greens V

MAKES 2
GENEROUS
PORTIONS

600ml chicken or vegetable stock

100g brown rice

100g spring greens, kale or spinach, or a combination of all of them

2 eggs

2 tbsp lemon juice, plus extra to serve

plenty of black pepper, to serve

Avgolemono is a Greek egg and lemon soup, sometimes served as a sauce over cooked meats, but mostly served in bowls as a hearty, nourishing soup. It is the taste of my childhood, of late-night suppers after Sunday dinners, of Monday after-school snacks, of second bowls full. The smell reminds me of my parents' house, holidays with my Aunty Helen at her home in Plymouth, being chased by geese and ducks and reading Reader's Digest *in the downstairs bathroom, hiding from my rambunctious cousins and siblings. This version deviates from my original recipe, which can be found in* A Girl Called Jack, *as it uses brown rice in place of white rice and has added greenery. It's just as rich and hearty and comforting as the original, but with some bonus extra vitamins and whole grains, too.*

First, bring your stock to the boil in a large saucepan. Pour in the rice and reduce the heat to a simmer for 30 minutes on the smallest hob ring, until it is soft and falling apart.

While the rice is cooking, finely chop your spring greens or kale, discarding the tough stalk, or roughly chop your spinach.

Crack the eggs into a mug or small bowl and add the lemon juice. Beat well to combine, then add a tablespoon of the hot stock, from the pan, to the mug. Beat well, adding a tablespoon at a time and combining completely before adding the next one. Do not rush this step, it is important that the eggs come to a warmer temperature gradually, else they will scramble, and then you lose the underpinning velvety texture of the whole dish for the sake of a few seconds' patience. When the mug is almost full, pour the contents slowly back into the saucepan, mixing well. Drop the greens in and fold through, warming them until they soften.

Serve immediately, with extra lemon juice and black pepper.

Will keep in the fridge for 2 days – ensure it is completely cool before chilling, then reheat until piping hot throughout to serve. Not recommended for freezing.

Avgolemono is synonymous with nurture, care and the cosy warmth of being well fed and satiated.

Chicken Porridge

SERVES 1

1 fat chicken thigh, skin on

1 tbsp oil

1 large onion

4 fat cloves of garlic

½ tsp dried thyme or dried mixed herbs

500ml water

40g porridge oats

lemon juice, to taste

black pepper, to taste

I have been fixated with the idea of chicken porridge for some years now, since reading an old Iranian recipe for it in a cookery book that I have not been able to locate since. My version is made by slow-cooking chicken thighs, then slow-cooking the oats in the resulting stock and juices. It's not strictly a ten-minute meal, but does require no more than ten minutes of effort and some idle babysitting, so it sort of counts. Hearty, creamy nursery food, everyone I have given it to try has recoiled and grimaced at the name and then asked for seconds after they've finished .... For a vegan version, omit the chicken thigh entirely and use a vegan chicken-style stock, like Osem, stirring through a drizzle of light oil to replicate the succulence of the original recipe.

Place your chicken thigh in a nonstick pan set on a medium hob over high heat. Add the oil, and cook until the skin is crisp and the thigh is sealed all over. Transfer to a heavy-bottomed saucepan and cover with the water.

Peel and finely slice your onion and add to the pan. Peel your garlic, quarter the cloves lengthways and add those too. Measure in the herbs and bring to the boil. Reduce to a simmer, cover and cook for an hour. Indulgent, I know, but essential here to extract all of the flavour and succulence that this recipe requires.

Remove the chicken thigh from the stock. Set aside the skin (see Tip opposite) and strip the meat from the bone. It should shred finely. Set it to one side.

Measure the oats into the stock and move the pan to the smallest hob over the lowest heat. Warm through for 15 minutes, stirring continuously, as the oats swell and soften. Add a splash of water to loosen as needed.

Stir through your shredded chicken and finish with lemon juice. Season to taste with black pepper to serve.

If you have leftovers, you can store them in the fridge for 24 hours. Loosen with a splash of milk or water as it will thicken more as it cools, then once completely cold, store in the fridge in a clean, airtight container. Reheat thoroughly to serve. Not recommended for freezing.

TIP

- *I deep-fry the skin then salt it and serve it on top, like a crisp, but I appreciate that this may be a step too far for some people.*

Cheese and Thyme Savoury Rice Pudding

SERVES 4

2 tbsp oil, or 1 tbsp each oil and butter

1 large onion, sliced, or 120g frozen sliced onions

6–12 fat cloves of garlic, to taste, or 3 tbsp garlic paste

180g brown rice

1 litre chicken stock

1 tsp dried mixed herbs or thyme

100g any kind of cheese

20g hard strong cheese

400ml full-fat milk

salt and pepper, to taste

'Not quite legitimately a risotto, but in need of a name that entices you into its evocative, creamy embrace' is what I scrawled in the margin of this recipe in one of my many handwritten notebooks that are all half-full and haphazardly disorganized. It was in the same notebook, some nine years earlier, I had scribbled down notes while watching Nigel Slater on the television. Nigel was making a cheese and thyme soufflé with thyme picked from his garden and a handful of ingredients. I watched, and listened, and wrote it down, intending to make it later on in the week. I still never have, partly because I have never made a soufflé, and I'm reluctant to make my first foray something I have been dreaming of for so long. I'd be devastated if I got it wrong, and so it remains a fantasy, buried in piles of words. Instead, I have borrowed those flavours for this. I have sometimes enriched it with an egg yolk beaten through the stock halfway through, to give the rich, thick base of an avgolemono, and it is very fine, but doesn't freeze quite as well and is an extra step of work, so I haven't included it in the main recipe.

Warm the oil or oil and butter in a large nonstick pan, and add the onion. Peel and roughly chop the garlic and season with a little salt and pepper. Cook over low heat for a few minutes, then stir in the rice.

Add half the chicken stock and the herbs, then bring to the boil. Cover and reduce to a simmer for 30 minutes, adding more stock as needed, stirring intermittently.

GOOD FOOD FOR BAD DAYS

Add any remaining stock, then turn the heat down very low. Grate in the cheeses, reserving some to serve. Stir well, and add the milk. Simmer over a very low heat for another 15 minutes, until thick and creamy. Keep an eye on the milk to ensure it doesn't boil over or spoil, and remove from the heat immediately if it starts to go.

Serve hot with the remaining cheese scattered on top and sprinkled with extra black pepper to serve.

It will keep in the fridge for 2 days. Cool completely before chilling, then reheat thoroughly to serve. Not recommended for freezing.

A variation on one-pan meals, here are some ideas for dishes to throw into the oven and leave them be. They are infinitely variable, so you can swap beans or meats or veggies for anything similar depending on what you like and what you have available.

There is a certain relief that comes with flinging a tray or a dish in the oven and walking away from it; no mindless stirring, no babysitting overboiling pots, no watchful eyes required; you can just abandon it and get on with something else instead. I very rarely use my oven; most of my meals I make at home are one-pan sling-ins or shoved in the slow cooker, but when I do, I always vow to do more of it. Stick it in, shut the door, walk away. Absolute bliss.

IN THE OVEN

Fish Crumble

SERVES 2 AS A
MAIN, 4 AS A
LIGHT LUNCH

2 tbsp cooking oil

2 tbsp plain flour

350ml milk

4 tbsp cheese

1 tsp mustard, any

1 x 125g tin of
mackerel,
preferably in brine

1 x 145g tin of tuna,
preferably in brine

1 x 290g tin of peas

1 x 300g tin of
sliced carrots

2 slices of bread

1 tbsp lemon juice

salt and pepper, to
taste

This recipe is a different take on a fish pie – a simpler one, as fish pie can be quite an undertaking, and although the end result is homely and comforting, the manner by which it is achieved seems to dirty every pan in my kitchen and exhaust every one of my nerves. And so I wanted to make a less challenging version, one that was just as satisfying but easier to assemble. Fish and breadcrumbs are a natural pairing – from fish fingers to fishcakes – and the contrast here between the creamy soft filling and the crunchy topping is simply lovely. You can use any tinned fish you fancy and replace the veg or bolster it with sweetcorn or jarred artichokes.

First, make your cheese sauce, so it's done and out of the way. Heat a little oil in a medium saucepan over low heat and quickly stir in the flour to form a thick paste. To prevent this from burning, I use the smallest hob ring and work quickly. Add a splash of the milk to loosen it, beating quickly. Repeat until all the milk has been worked into the sauce and it is smooth and lump-free. Add the cheese and mustard, and turn the heat up slightly to melt it, still stirring. Season with salt and pepper and set to one side to cool and thicken.

Open your mackerel, tuna, peas and carrots and drain each well. If either of the fish are in oil, instead of brine, strain it into a small jar and pop it in the fridge to use for cooking – it adds an umami (savoury) base to onions for puttanesca, for example, or for frying fish in. I keep all of mine in neat little jars like sentries

CONTINUES OVER THE PAGE →

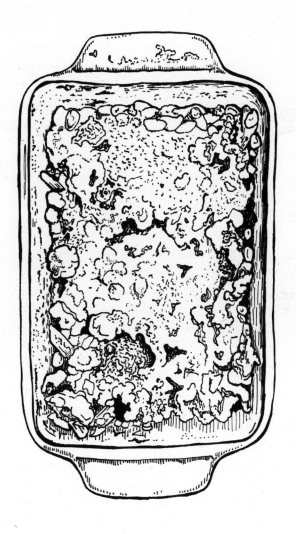

in the fridge door, labelled with the date of decanting, and instructions to use within 2 weeks. Add the fish and vegetables to the cheese sauce in the pan and fold through gently.

Grate the bread into crumbs, or pulse in a small blender if you have one. Spoon the fish, veg and sauce into a small ovenproof tin – a 450g loaf tin or 20cm cake tin is perfect. Top with the breadcrumbs and sprinkle lemon juice on top. Finish with a very generous scattering of black pepper. Bake in the oven at 180°C/160°C fan/gas 4 for 15 minutes to warm through and toast the top, and serve hot.

Will keep in the fridge for 2 days, covered, or freeze in portions in freezerproof containers for up to 3 months. Defrost completely in the fridge overnight, then microwave to piping hot throughout to serve.

Stewed Steak Lasagne

SERVES 4-6

200g onion (about 2 medium onions)

2 x 400g tins of chopped tomatoes

2 tbsp peeled and chopped garlic or garlic paste

1 tsp dried mixed herbs

200ml red or white wine

2 x 400g tins of stewed steak

1 x 400g tin of brown lentils

400–500g lasagne sheets

2 balls of mozzarella, or 200g Cheddar cheese

salt and pepper, to taste

I'll be the first to admit that this is an absolute travesty of a complete classic, but it's also very quick and surprisingly delicious, and it dispenses with most of the faff of making a traditional lasagne.

First, preheat your oven to 180°C/160°C fan/gas 4 and get your lasagne dish – something square or rectangular and fairly deep is ideal, a loaf tin will do at a pinch.

Peel and finely slice the onion and toss into a large nonstick pan with the tomatoes, garlic, herbs and wine. Season with a little salt and pepper, and cook over medium heat for around 15 minutes, until the onions start to soften and the liquid reduces.

Open the tins of stewed steak and tip into the pan, along with the thick gravy. Drain and thoroughly rinse the lentils and add those too. Warm through briefly.

Spread a layer of steak-tomato mix into your dish. Top with lasagne sheets. Repeat until the steak mix has almost run out – you need to reserve some for the top layer as the wetness is what cooks the lasagne sheets. Top with the remaining mixture. Slice the mozzarella or grate your Cheddar cheese and layer over the top of the meat.

Cover with foil and bake in the oven for 30 minutes until the cheese has melted and the pasta has cooked through – a small sharp knife inserted into the centre should pass through with minimal resistance. Remove the foil and cook for 10 more minutes to brown and crisp the cheese on top, and serve.

Will keep in the fridge for 2–3 days, tightly covered. Not recommended for freezing. Reheat thoroughly before serving.

Sticky Beer and Lime Chicken with Vegetable Rice

SERVES 2

½ fresh lime, or
1 tbsp lime juice

1 tbsp honey

1 tbsp soy sauce

1 tbsp light cooking
oil

250ml beer, any

2 large chicken
breasts or 4 thighs
and drumsticks,
skin on

1 large red or white
onion

½ bulb of fennel
(optional)

2 medium carrots

150g brown rice

This one-tray dinner is super simple and makes enough for two meals with very little effort. The juices from the chicken flavour the rice, along with the beer and the sweet-sour-salty marinade. Beer and lime are a classic pairing, and this easy, hearty dinner is impressive enough to make you feel like you've made a real effort for yourself.

First, preheat your oven to 190°C/170°C fan/gas 5 and find a medium-sized roasting dish. You'll need to cover this while the dish cooks, so get out some tin foil or find a baking tray or sheet that fits neatly over the top of it – it doesn't matter if it overlaps around the edges, as long as it all fits in the oven.

Mix together the lime juice, honey, soy sauce, oil and 1 tablespoon of the beer in a bowl large enough to hold the chicken. Place the chicken in – skin-side down if using thighs, plump side down if using breasts. Set to one side to marinate.

Peel and finely slice the onion and toss it into the roasting dish. Grate in the fennel, if using, and the carrots, then mix it all up a bit. Measure in the rice, and add the rest of the beer, slowly so it doesn't fizz up the sides! Stir well.

Place the chicken on top, reserving any leftover marinade to use later. Cover with foil or the baking sheet and place in the oven for 45 minutes.

Remove from the oven, then baste the chicken with the leftover marinade. Pour the rest over the rice, if you like. Return to the oven, uncovered, for 10 minutes to finish cooking. Serve immediately as a hot meal, or allow to cool completely and eat fridge-cold.

Sausage, Squash and Apple Traybake

**SERVES 2,
GENEROUSLY, OR 4
AS A LIGHT MEAL
WITH SIDES**

1 small red or white
onion

6–8 fat sausages

1 large apple, any
kind

160g frozen
butternut squash
chunks

1–2 tbsp cooking oil

1–2 tbsp balsamic
vinegar, or 2 tsp red
wine vinegar, and
1 tsp honey

2 tsp dried mixed
herbs, or dried
thyme or sage

plenty of black
pepper

*This is absolutely mindless comfort food; the squash
and apple almost self-mash as the sausages and onion
caramelize, creating a bounty of soft, sweet, sticky
flavour. If you use frozen veg, the only prep needed is to
chop up the apple, the rest is just bundled into a roasting
tin and left to do its thing. For extra veg, add some torn
kale, with the hard stalk removed, three minutes before
serving. Frozen will work here too, but add it six minutes
before the end to give it a chance to defrost. A whole meal
by itself, but also delicious cold with pasta or hot on a pile
of buttery mash or greens – or both.*

First, heat your oven to 180°C/160°C fan/gas 4 and ensure there is
a shelf in the middle or just below.

Peel your onion and halve it, then cut each half into thirds. Place
in a roasting dish and add the sausages.

Core and cut the apple the same way and add to the dish, along
with the frozen chunks of squash. Give it all a jiggle to evenly
distribute the ingredients.

Drizzle with the oil and vinegar, or vinegar and honey mix, and
scatter over the herbs and black pepper. Bake in the centre of the
oven for 40 minutes, shaking gently halfway through.

Will keep, cooled and stored in an airtight bag or container, for up
to 3 days in the fridge. Not recommended for freezing.

Cauliflower Cheese and White Bean Bake

SERVES 4, GENEROUSLY

1 large onion, or 120g frozen diced onions

1 tbsp cooking oil, plus extra for greasing

1 x 400g tin of butter beans

1 x 400g tin of cannellini beans

500ml chicken stock, or water and 1 stock cube

½ tsp mustard, any

a pinch of grated nutmeg

1 large head of cauliflower, or 450g frozen cauli florets

120g mature Cheddar, or similar

2 slices of bread, blitzed or grated to crumbs, or 4 tbsp dried breadcrumbs

salt and pepper, to taste

This is the ultimate in comfort food – cauliflower cheese reinvented as a legitimate meal. It's just as comforting as the original, but with a touch more protein and a crisp breadcrumb topping. For a more substantial meal I sometimes add cooked brown rice – just boil it in a separate pan while the first one is cooking, then stir it through before baking. You'll need a bigger dish to accommodate it, though!

First peel and finely slice your onion and add to a large nonstick pan, or shake in the frozen onions if using those instead. Add a tablespoon of oil and a pinch of salt and cook gently over low heat for 5 minutes to start to soften.

Drain and thoroughly rinse your beans and tip them into the pan. Cover with the stock (or water and a stock cube), then add the mustard and nutmeg. Bring to the boil, then reduce to a simmer for 20 minutes.

Turn your oven on to 180°C/160°C fan/gas 4 and make sure there is a shelf in the middle. (I often forget to check this and then have to try to manouevre it when it's hotter than Hades, so just a gentle reminder here, and I hope that it isn't instruction overkill.) Lightly grease a decent-sized ovenproof dish – mine is 20cm x 20cm, so anything around this size, or a medium cake tin or pie dish, will do.

Remove the outer leaves of your cauliflower. Cut the heavy stalk from the bottom and chop the cauli into small florets – as a rough guide, the top should be no bigger than a 50p piece so they cook evenly. It makes it easier to eat as well! Add the cauli to the pan and stir through. Cover to retain as much of the remaining liquid as possible, then cook for 15 minutes, or until the cauli is soft and a fork gently prodded into it goes through with little to no resistance.

Tip the contents of the pan into your prepared dish. Grate cheese over the veg and top with breadcrumbs. Bake in the oven for 10 minutes to crisp the crumbs and melt the cheese, then serve immediately with extra black pepper on top.

Will keep in the fridge for up to 3 days, covered or stored in an airtight container. Reheat to piping hot to serve. Not recommended for freezing due to the high dairy content – you can, but it doesn't show it at its best!

Sometimes when you're down in the dumps, or having a bad day, or just low on energy, if you're anything like me, only a saccharine sugar hit will do. Too much of it can have a negative impact on your mental and physical health, but I'm a firm believer that a little bit of what you fancy can do the world of good sometimes.

I keep a Kilner jar of Pick 'n' Mix in my office at home for quick fixes in a slump, but there's nothing quite like the smell of freshly baked biscuits or cake to make you feel comforted and slightly more relaxed. Maybe it's a childhood thing, reminiscent of apple turnovers scoffed in the car, still warm from my Home Economics class, giggling with my dad or standing stirring Christmas cake mixture with my mum's arms around me, both of us holding the spoon and making a wish. Whatever it is, the following simple recipes are some of my favourites – some old classics and some new delights, to give you a little boost on a bluesy day.

THE SWEET STUFF

Lemon Curd No-Churn Ice Cream v

MAKES 1 DECENT-SIZED TUB

2 x 400g tins of full-fat coconut milk

200g lemon curd

This ice cream is closer in texture to a soft-serve semifreddo, with a subtle hint of lemon underpinned by the dense creaminess of the coconut milk. I decided to try to make it as an experiment; lemon curd contains almost all of the fundamental ingredients used to make traditional ice cream, like sugar and eggs, and was pleased to find it worked beautifully. I have also made it with grapefruit curd, which is absolutely delightful but harder to find in supermarkets. Low-fat coconut milk just won't work here, this is one of the rare occasions where only the really thick, fatty stuff will do.

First chill your coconut milk in the fridge overnight, so the thick coconut cream separates from the clear coconut water.

When well chilled, open the cans. Spoon the firm, white coconut cream into the large cup of a bullet blender or ordinary blender or food processor. Add the lemon curd and pulse to combine.

Pour the coconut-lemon mixture into an ice-cube tray and pop it in the freezer for 4 hours to set, scraping as much as you can from the blades and the inside of the blender.

When the ice cream is set, pop the cubes out and back into the blender. Pulse briefly to combine them, then scrape it into a Tupperware container and return to the freezer for 15 minutes.

Serve immediately, or remove from the freezer 10 minutes before you wish to serve to allow it to soften.

Sleazecake V

MAKES 4 SMALL
CAKES

100g ginger biscuits

1 x 410g tin of pear
halves in syrup

200g soft cream
cheese

200g thick Greek
yoghurt

4 tbsp icing sugar or
caster sugar

honey, for drizzling

*Not quite the baked, creamy succulence of a traditional
cheesecake, but a reasonable substitute in a hurry.*

Pop the biscuits in a freezer bag and smash up with a rolling pin
until they resemble big breadcrumbs, or break them up into the
large cup of a bullet blender and pulse to smithereens. Transfer
the biscuit crumbs to a small mixing bowl and spoon in a
tablespoon of the syrup from the tin of pears. Stir quickly to
combine, adding another tablespoon if required.

Divide the biscuit base between four ramekins or glasses, and
push it down firmly with your fingers to compact it.

Blend two-thirds of the pears – not the remaining juice or syrup
– with the cream cheese, Greek yoghurt and sugar. Spoon
carefully into each glass or ramekin. Top with a slice or two of
pear and a drizzle of honey. Chill in the fridge for at least an hour
for best results – can be eaten right away but it's better when it's
set a little.

Keeps for 24–48 hours in the fridge, covered. Not recommended
for freezing.

Ice Cream Cake v

MAKES 1 LARGE LOAF CAKE, ABOUT 8 GENEROUS SLICES

410g ice cream

oil, for greasing

215g self-raising flour

1½ tsp baking powder

Ice cream is my catch-all, cheer-up indulgence, eaten by the pint in front of light comedic television or crime-scene dramas, depending on my mood. One Saturday evening, alone, I found myself partway down a tub of Ben & Jerry's, wondering if I could use it as a substitute for the majority of ingredients in a traditional cake recipe. Ice cream is, after all, made from eggs, fat and sugar, all key building blocks in a standard sponge. I pottered to the kitchen with it in hand and set it on the worktop to melt – an act of extraordinary willpower, if I may congratulate myself briefly for it, as I have been known to eat two tubs back to back. A little maths and some crossed fingers later, and I was tucking into an atrociously light chocolate loaf cake, made with just two ingredients and a dash of incredulity. I added the baking powder to a later edition, and it was even better, so I'm including it here.

I later learned that I was not the first person to try this; readers sent me their own ideas for Smarties ice-cream cake, and I made a slightly complicated Neapolitan traybake after Emily Leary, who writes the award-winning food and parenting blog 'A Mummy Too', suggested it in the late hours of the evening. Flavours I have experimented with so far have included Ben & Jerry's Half Baked, cheap vanilla, raspberry ripple and mint choc chip – the latter is my son's favourite, especially drenched in squeezy chocolate sauce.

GOOD FOOD FOR BAD DAYS

Remove your ice cream from the freezer and leave it to melt completely, which usually takes around an hour. Don't be tempted to speed up this process by heating it up, as that changes how it reacts in the recipe and your cake may not work as well. This is a great use for ice cream that has melted beyond redemption, accidentally left out of the freezer, as well.

Preheat your oven to 180°C/160°C fan/gas 4, and set the shelf slightly below the centre. Lightly grease a 450g loaf tin. Spoon your ice cream into a mixing bowl and add half of the flour. Add in the baking powder and mix well to form a runny batter.

Add the remaining flour a heaped tablespoon at a time, mixing it in well until it is all incorporated into the mixture. The batter may be unusually thick, depending on the ice cream used; this is completely normal at this stage.

Spoon and scrape every last drop of the cake mixture into the loaf tin, and smooth the top. It doesn't have to be perfect, but the mixture is so thick it may need a gentle nudge into the corners!

Place the loaf tin in the oven and bake for 35–40 minutes, until risen and a small sharp knife or cocktail stick or skewer inserted into the middle comes out clean. If it is still a little sticky, return it to the oven for 10 minutes, turning the heat down to 140°C/120°C fan/gas 1 to keep the top from burning.

When your cake is cooked, remove it from the oven and cool in the tin for 15 minutes. Gently turn out to serve hot or cold.

This cake will keep for 3 days, tightly wrapped in cling film or tin foil and stored in an airtight container. To freeze it, slice it thickly and place each piece in a food storage bag. Defrost thoroughly, then warm through to serve.

'Jaffa Cake' Mug Pudding V

SERVES 1

2 tbsp marmalade, plus extra to finish

2 tbsp Nutella or other chocolate spread, plus extra to finish

3 tbsp vegetable oil

3 tbsp milk

1 egg

2 tbsp honey or sugar

4 tbsp self-raising flour

squeezy chocolate sauce, or more chocolate spread, to serve

This is a very dangerous piece of knowledge to have; the ability to rustle up a hot sticky pudding in a matter of minutes that tastes like a pile of melted Jaffa cakes. Once you know it, you can never un-know it, and I'm very glad to finally share it with you.

First measure the marmalade and chocolate spread into your mug, and pop it into the microwave for 45 seconds to soften.

Remove carefully as the mug may be warm, and stir in the oil, then the milk. Leave to cool for a minute or two before cracking in the egg and beating it well. Mix in the honey, or sugar if using, and then the flour, to make your batter.

Place the mug back in the microwave for 90 seconds on High. It will rise quite a bit, but it deflates again a little afterward.

Top with an extra smudge of marmalade and chocolate spread, then return to the microwave for 30 seconds more to melt them and finish cooking the pudding.

Remove, and allow to stand for a minute or two before tucking in as it will be hot!

I like to top mine with squeezy chocolate sauce as well, because I don't know when enough is enough, really.

It doesn't keep particularly brilliantly, so it's best to eat it soon after making it.

Sticky Grapefruit Honey Squares V

**MAKES 9 HEFTY OR
16 REASONABLE-
SIZED SQUARES**

1 x 540g tin of
grapefruit (you need
150g drained weight)

250g natural yoghurt

2 medium eggs

180g runny honey

1 tsp vanilla extract

60ml light cooking
oil, plus extra for
greasing

300g plain flour

2 tsp baking powder

These cakes are dense and sticky, a homage to the honey-drenched cakes I enjoyed from many Cypriot relatives and family friends in my youth. Theirs were studded with crumbled walnuts and pistachios; I have opted to spike mine with the lip-smacking tartness of tinned grapefruit. The honey syrup is mandatory; the cake just isn't the same without it.

Preheat your oven to 160°C/140°C fan/gas 3 and set a shelf just below the centre. Lightly grease a 20cm x 20cm cake tin.

Place a fine-mesh strainer over a large bowl and drain the grapefruit well. Press the segments down gently with your fingers to extract as much juice as possible. Reserve the juice – you'll need it later.

Weigh out 150g drained grapefruit into the large cup of a bullet blender. Add the yoghurt, eggs, 120g of the honey, the vanilla and the oil. Blend to a smooth liquid and set to one side.

Weigh your flour and measure your baking powder into a large mixing bowl, and pour in the grapefruit-yoghurt liquid. Mix well to make a loose, frothy batter. The froth is the reaction between the acidic juices in the grapefruit and the baking powder – it settles back down after a minute.

Pour the cake batter into the greased tin and bake in the centre of the oven for 50 minutes, until risen and firm. It will be considerably denser than a standard cake – and it's about to get even more so.

Remove from the oven and allow to cool for 10 minutes in the tin. While it is cooling, warm the remaining honey and grapefruit juice and mix well together to make the syrup.

Cut the cake into squares, still in the tin. Pierce all over with a cocktail stick, around 60 times. Pour the honey syrup liberally over the top and let it soak into the cake as it cools.

Serve warm or cool or heat through to piping hot, it's enjoyable every way. Keeps for 3 days in an airtight container – best stored in the fridge.

Hot Apple Pies v

MAKES 8 SMALL PIES

1 packet ready-made puff pastry, approx 325g

1 tsp ground cinnamon

1 jar of applesauce

light cooking oil, such as vegetable oil, for frying

sugar (optional)

Not unlike the hot apple pies made popular by a huge fast-food chain! You can make your own applesauce for these if you'd rather, but in a hurry, the jars of applesauce from the supermarket will do just fine.

Roll out your puff pastry to 3mm thick and, using a ruler, cut it into eight equal-sized rectangles. The easiest way to do this is to cut it in half across the middle, then into four, top to bottom.

Stir the cinnamon into the applesauce. Dollop the applesauce mixture into the top half of each rectangle and carefully fold the bottom up so the bottom edge meets the top edge. Seal the edges by pressing them together with a fork, and use a large sharp knife to trim them so they are even all the way round. Keep the pastry offcuts to test the oil with later.

Carefully transfer the pies to a plate and chill them in the fridge for 30 minutes to firm up.

When the pies are chilled, bring a medium-sized saucepan, half-filled with light cooking oil to medium heat. When small bubbles start to appear, drop a piece of the offcut pastry into the pan. If it puffs up and floats to the top within a few seconds, the oil is ready. If it doesn't, watch it carefully for a minute or two more and try again. If at any point the pan starts to smoke, remove it from the heat immediately and carry it outside to cool down. Do not take your eye off it and always, always supervise it.

When the oil is ready, turn the heat down low to prevent it from overheating, and line a plate with kitchen roll or a clean kitchen towel. Carefully lower a pie into the pan on a turner or slotted spoon. Cook for 5 minutes, until golden and crisp, then remove quickly onto the plate. Repeat until all the pies are cooked. Sprinkle with sugar, if you like, and serve hot.

The pies will keep, cooked or uncooked, in the fridge for 3 days. If uncooked, store them on a plate wrapped in cling film. If cooked, they can be piled into a Tupperware container. Uncooked pies can also be frozen for up to 3 months and defrosted fully before cooking as above.

For a healthier pie, you can bake them in the oven, glazed with a beaten egg and cooked at 190°C/170°C fan/gas 5 for 15 minutes, or until golden and crisp.

Brown Rice Pudding V

MAKES 4 PORTIONS

1 litre water

160g brown rice

700ml full-fat milk

4 tbsp honey

½ tsp ground cinnamon

a pinch of grated nutmeg (optional)

Brown rice has a bit of a reputation for being tough to cook, but this rice pudding couldn't be simpler. The end result is worth the long, slow cook – it falls apart with a gentle suck, collapsing into an ambrosial creamy nursery food that's a heart-soothing remedy for the bleakest of days.

Measure the water into a large saucepan, preferably a nonstick one, and place it on your largest hob ring. Bring it to the boil.

Pour in the brown rice, then move the pan to the smallest hob ring. It seems a bit of a faff, I know, but it will give you the best results. Pour in half of the milk, then add the honey, cinnamon and nutmeg, if using.

Simmer on the lowest heat for 30 minutes, adding the remaining milk as the rice absorbs it, stirring occasionally to release the starch and make it creamy and stop it sticking to the bottom of the pan.

It will be ready to eat after 30 minutes, however, for best results cook it very gently for another half an hour, adding more milk as you need to, as it will break down further into a collapsing creamy dish reminiscent of tinned rice pudding.

Sweeten to taste with more honey as desired, and serve.

Will keep in the fridge for 2 days; ensure it is completely cool before chilling, and reheat until piping hot throughout to serve. Not recommended for freezing.

The Ambassador's Brownies V

**MAKES 4
PORTIONS.
ALLEGEDLY**

50g butter

50g your favourite
peanut butter

50g Nutella or other
chocolate spread

100g honey or sugar

18g cocoa powder

1 egg

50g plain flour

These are named after a dessert I love at Hawksmoor, my friend Fiona's son Ben's resplendent group of restaurants, which I have visited three times on special occasions. Theirs is a chocolate and hazelnut bombe of ice cream wrapped in gold leaf and dusted with hazelnuts, cheekily called Ambassador's Reception after a certain favourite after-dinner chocolate. I've borrowed the concept and made it into five-minute brownies that can be cooked in the microwave, so be warned, once you read this recipe, you're never more than five minutes away from fudgy paradise. It should serve four, but routinely, it does not.

First, find a bowl that will hold your brownie; I use a wide, shallow pasta bowl for best results.

Measure in your butter, peanut butter and Nutella or chocolate spread and place in the microwave. Cook on High for 45 seconds to melt the ingredients. Remove carefully, as the bowl may be hot, and stir well to combine.

Stir in the honey or sugar, then the cocoa powder. This will cool the mixture slightly so the egg doesn't scramble! Break in the egg, and mix well with a fork to thoroughly beat it in. Finally, stir in the flour to form a smooth, glossy batter. Return the bowl to the microwave and cook for 4 minutes on High.

Remove carefully and leave the bowl to stand for 15 minutes to continue to cook, and to cool slightly.

Keeps in the fridge for 2 days, or freeze for 3 months. Defrost in the fridge overnight and reheat until piping hot throughout.

Silent Courgette Cake VE

MAKES 8 HEFTY SLICES

2 large courgettes

80ml light cooking oil, plus extra for greasing

8 tbsp marmalade

1 small lemon or lime

250g self-raising flour

80g sugar

40g cocoa powder

My Small Boy, who is ten years old and increasingly wise to my wily ways with vegetables, adores this cake. The courgettes are smuggled in, disappearing in their blandness, to lend a moist, almost fudgy texture. It is, incidentally, vegan as well, the marmalade replacing eggs in some miraculous twist of science. I'd go as far as to suggest that a cake made entirely of plants is practically a salad, if you need any further convincing; it's what I tell myself when my child has seconds, anyway.

First, preheat your oven to 180°C/160°C fan/gas 4, and lightly grease a 900g loaf tin.

Dice your courgettes and pop them into your blender, along with the oil and the marmalade. Zest the lemon or lime into the mix, and then halve it and juice it rigorously, until it has nothing left to give. If you don't have a lemon squeezer, you can work it out with a fork and some elbow grease, or by digging your (clean) thumbs in and shoving them around a bit. When the citrus is a husk of its former self, discard it and blend the wet ingredients to a smooth liquid. Set to one side, you'll need these in a moment.

Weigh the flour, sugar and cocoa powder into a large mixing bowl, and stir well to combine evenly. Pour the wet ingredients into the centre, scraping out the blender jug or cup thoroughly to get as much of it as possible. Mix well to form a smooth batter – there may be a moment where you think it's too dry, but persevere and it will work out in the end.

Spoon the batter into the prepared loaf tin and place on the centre shelf of the oven. Bake for 45 minutes, or until a small sharp knife or skewer inserted into the centre comes out clean. If any cake sticks to the knife, return it to the oven for 10 more minutes to finish off.

When cooked, remove from the oven and cool in the tin for 30 minutes, before turning out and slicing. For best results, allow it to cool for a further 30 minutes on a wire rack, but I know that freshly baked cake is irresistible, so if you don't mind the risk of a slight crumbly edge, dig in.

It will keep for 3 days, well wrapped in an airtight container, or 3 months in the freezer.

Black Forest Traybake V

MAKES 9 HEFTY
SQUARES, 12
REASONABLE-SIZED
RECTANGLES OR 16
BITE-SIZED
SQUARES, ETC.

200g butter

200g red jam

3 medium eggs

2–4 tbsp cocoa
powder, to taste

1 tsp baking powder

200g self-raising
flour

100g dark chocolate

200g fresh or frozen
blackberries or
cherries

I use jam in place of the traditional sugar in this traybake, which makes it slightly fudgy in texture. It may need a little longer to cook depending on which jam you use – generally the fancier the jam, the higher the fruit content, so it takes a little longer to cook through. Low-sugar and sugar-free jams are very tricky to make work here, when I tested them the finished result was more like a sloppy brownie than a traybake, which isn't a bad thing, just not what I was going for! Test by inserting a knife, skewer or piece of dried spaghetti in the centre. If it comes out clean, it's done, but if it's sticky, cover it with foil to prevent the top from browning, turn the heat down to 150°C/130°C fan/gas 2 and pop back in the oven for 10 minutes or so.

First, heat your oven to 180°C/160°C fan/gas 4 and ensure there is a shelf in the centre or just below. Lightly grease a 20cm square cake tin or one of a similar volume.

Weigh out your butter and jam into a large mixing bowl and beat together briskly to cream them into an even-coloured paste. Add one egg and mix well to incorporate, then repeat with the remaining two eggs, beating until smooth.

Spoon in the cocoa powder, then the baking powder, and mix well. Add the flour, a third at a time, incorporating it all before adding the next lot.

When the batter is smooth, even and glossy, break the chocolate into squares and fold through with the berries or cherries.

Pour the batter into the prepared tin and bake for 50 minutes. Cool in the tin for 15 minutes before slicing into squares to serve.

Will keep in an airtight container for 4 days, or in the freezer for 3 months. Defrost completely overnight in the fridge or at room temperature, and reheat thoroughly to serve.

TIP

- *If I'm extremely tight on time or low on energy, I simply sling all of the ingredients except for the flour and berries in the large cup of my bullet blender or my rickety 1980s food processor. Blitz to smooth, then scrape into a mixing bowl and stir in the flour and berries. It's faster, smoother, but does generate a little extra washing up.*

Notes

1   Li, B., Lv, J., Wang, W. & Zhang, D. (2017) Dietary magnesium and calcium intake and risk of depression in the general population: A meta-analysis. *The Australian and New Zealand Journal of Psychiatry*, 51(3), pp.219–29

2   Tuenter, E., Foubert, K. & Pieters, L. (2018) Mood Components in Cocoa and Chocolate: The Mood Pyramid. *Planta Medica*, 84 (12–14), pp.839–44

3   Young, S. (2007) Folate and Depression – A neglected problem. *Journal of Psychiatry and Neuroscience*, 32(2), pp.80–82

4   Wang, J., Um, P., Dickerman, B.A. & Liu, J. (2018) Zinc, Magnesium, Selenium and Depression: A Review of the Evidence, Potential Mechanisms and Implications. *Nutrients*, 10(5), p.584

5   Larrieu, T. & Layé, S. (2018) Food for Mood: Relevance of Nutritional Omega-3 Fatty Acids for Depression and Anxiety. *Frontiers in Physiology*, 9, p.1047

Index

About Jack

Jack Monroe is an award-winning food writer and bestselling author. Books include *A Girl Called Jack*, *A Year In 120 Recipes*, *Cooking On A Bootstrap*, *Tin Can Cook* and *Vegan (ish)*. She has won the Fortnum & Mason Food and Drink Award (ironically); the Observer Food Monthly Best Food Blog and Food Personality Of The Year; Marie Claire 'Woman At The Top'; Red Magazine's 'Red Hot Women'; the YMCA Courage & Inspiration Award; the Woman Of The Year Entrepreneur Award; the Women Of The Future Media Award and many more. She works with and supports The Trussell Trust, Child Poverty Action Group, Plan Zheroes, The Food Chain and countless food banks, schools and children's centres to teach people to cook and eat well on a low income, and campaigns against the causes of poverty and austerity in Britain and abroad. She lives in Southend on Sea, Essex, with her partner and son, and a large ginger cat.

Thanks

With thanks, as ever, to Rosemary Scoular and Natalia Lucas at United Agents. To Carole Tonkinson, Martha Burley, Jodie Mullish, Zainab Dawood, Jess Duffy, Sian Gardiner, Hockley Raven Spare, and Mel Four at Bluebird. To Patricia Niven for her photography and generous heart. To Jill Tytherleigh for the beautiful illustrations that bring my recipes to life, and Matt Haig for the foreword, and such kindness. To Kris, for everything, including but not limited to our tiny incredible human. To my parents, for their endless if bewildered support of my bonkers life and accidental career. To Louisa, for bringing me crisp sandwiches on my own bad days, and my son, Jonathon, for being my sunshine in the dark. And to you, dear reader, for picking up this book. May we all have good days ahead of us.